STATION

STATION

A journey through 20th and 21st
century railway architecture and design

Christopher Beanland

BATSFORD

First published in the United Kingdom in 2024
by Batsford
43 Great Ormond Street
London WC1N 3HZ

An imprint of B. T. Batsford Holdings Limited

ISBN: 9781849948258

A CIP catalogue record for this book is
available from the British Library.

10 9 8 7 6 5 4 3 2 1

Reproduction by Rival Colour, UK
Printed and bound by Vivar Printing, Malaysia

This book can be ordered direct from the
publisher at www.batsfordbooks.com, or try
your local bookshop.

CONTENTS

Introduction

Imagine a world where every step was a trial, where mud and forest and things that eat you got between you and your destination, where horses cantered between inns and everyone smelled. The recent reality of our world was a place where – essentially – you didn't travel unless you had a good reason. Men off to make money or make love or make war took these bizarre Barry Lyndon journeys involving so much side plot. The only real way you could travel anywhere was on a boat – the land was unconquered.

I met my great-grandmother, a child of the 1800s, incredibly born when Queen Victoria was on the throne in the United Kingdom. Her mother knew this world, right on the point that Yorkshire industrialized and the world exploded, sending ripples down the decades. In the 1830s the world changed completely as the railway and the steam engine came to prominence in a flash of exuberance where pure chance and scientific skill somehow mixed in the white-hot embers of the fires of human imagination, pioneered in England's North at the Stockton and Darlington Railway, Middleton Railway in Leeds and the Liverpool to Manchester Railway.

When you live in a country whose past seems to offer more than its future, you learn these lessons in school, on TV every night, at preserved heritage railways on the weekend: the technology that shaped the world, Stephenson and Watt et al, were the mad Musks of their day, the nutty professors whose experiments bizarrely worked – even though there were many explosions, crashes and deaths to come.

And for my great-grandmother's mother, life would never be the same again: a fiery furnace of social changes; enclosure forcing the peasants from their common grazing land into Bradford's wool factories; the potato famine starving the Irish into the English mills; jobs and routines and clocks set by railway companies rather than the sun and the seasons; back-breaking graft, filth and horror and injury and mistreatment and repetition; but also the chance to make something in the mire – a distant relative (perhaps) mopped up all the building contracts in Bradford to construct the banks and the mills and villas. William Beanland lies immortalized in Undercliffe Cemetery, a member of the merchant class Marx and Engels were studying in Manchester as they watched the wretched poor slip further into

drink and prostitution and saw a revolution as the only corollary.

The industrial world needed to move people – the commuters on the trains. The railways brought people to work their dead-end jobs as it does today. The paper pushing is now key pushing, we convince ourselves the pointlessness has a worth – or we just accept it doesn't and take the money anyway.

But the railway also began to take the people away for pleasure: soon you could visit Scarborough and Whitby and Southport and even London. If time had changed so had distance: the possibilities stretched and required a new mental outlook. How could you live through an age like this? We baulk at the way technology super-speeds the changes today; one wonders if this rapid social change itself is one reason for the anxieties and the attention-deficit disorders you see in everyone if you look hard enough. Imagine how much therapy the Victorians would have needed – and how ill-equipped the workhouses and the asylums were to look after a people who were so shocked, who had gone from such a small life to such a restless one. The trains partly did this, a steam-powered jolt to the system.

For the next 100 years the railways dominated everything like a Bruce Forsyth on metal rails, refusing to go quietly or not be there every day: they were the ways you got around, they were for the military and the vacationers, for transporting people and for transporting the new goods and the coal and the wood needed to power everything. The railways bought everything up and opened more: hotels, factories, shops. The system reshaped the very land that sheep had grazed on for centuries: viaducts crossed valleys and in urban areas everything was pushed aside – the graves at St Pancras Old Churchyard were shifted by a young Thomas Hardy so the Midland Railway could plough through. Rails injected themselves everywhere like parasites. Thousands died building the follies – the graveyards on the moors above the Woodhead Tunnel in the Pennines mark the last resting place of the mainly Irish navvies whose death rates were higher than soldiers at the Battle of Waterloo. As well as the bulk cargos the trains were eventually given royal approval and ferried the elites around – Wolferton Station is preserved as a quaint reminder of when kings and queens would catch the royal train from London to Sandringham for every Christmas holiday.

Wars needed railways – indeed, many railways like those in Paris and Berlin's loop lines were constructed especially to allow military trains access to the lines out to various parts of the country. The First and Second World Wars were dominated by the vast bulk transports of fuels and ammunition on the rails, people too – lest we forget the horrors, increasing in scale from the troop trains carrying scared young boys to the fronts, to the refugee trains ferrying the displaced, to the outright catastrophe of the Nazi cattle trucks loaded with humans bound for the gas chambers. Trains had proved their worth – even if the intention often disgusted. And what did they get in return? The post-war age was to be the motor age, and then the age of flight.

For half of the 20th century hardly anyone was celebrating trains and stations; we were lost in a drunken fug of exhaust smoke and screeching tyres and motorway plans – the USA and Asia and Eastern Europe still are. Around the world railways were subjugated by the car: Birmingham New Street is essentially demolished to make way for a car park on top of it; Prague Hlavní Nádraží gets a motorway running right outside the front door and narrowly escapes the wrecking ball; Penn Station bulldozed and put underground; the Euston Arch taken down and thrown into the Lea. Grand Central was even nearly axed in the mid-1970s, if you can believe that. Jackie Kennedy's campaigning saved the station that we all recognize today as one of America's most beautiful.

East Dereham's bypass on the A47 road in Norfolk was laid on the course of a former railway, and the Cambridgeshire guided busway was laid on a former railway. LA had all its streetcar lines bought up and ripped up in one of the biggest municipal swindles in human history, which inspired the film *Who Framed Roger Rabbit*. The perpetrators? The oil, automobile and tyre corporations. The argument was often that the railway companies of the 19th century were too powerful – dominating everything. Now it was the turn of the auto industry. This was sold as personal emancipation – the idea that you were in control of your own vehicle and your own life, and timetables were no longer your boss.

The suburbanization of the United States was made possible by cars and the federal highway programmes that gave them roads to drive on; enabling white flight and building freeways like the Cross Bronx Expressway right through black neighbourhoods to boot. City planner Robert Moses got everything he wanted – almost. His Lower Manhattan Expressway was stopped by Jane Jacobs and the locals of Soho, Little Italy and Chinatown, as you can discover in my book *Unbuilt* (apologies for the product placement).

The USA went from around 40,000 stations at the peak of its railroad age to little more than 500 Amtrak halts, and every year the service suffers, despite the recently improved Acela trains on the East Coast. Argentina's rail map of the 19th century was impressively tentacular. As the 20th century went on, the majority of lines were removed. Ireland removed a vast swathe of lines and Australia did too.

As Zdeněk Tomeŝ points out, this decline – centred as it was more markedly than anywhere else in the Rust Belt of the USA – was also a problem of freight. Railways (and airlines) often joke that passengers are simply 'living cargo'. The real dosh is in freight. And deindustrialization in Detroit and Baltimore and Buffalo was a hammer blow. The railways made money transporting heavy bulky stuff like wood and steel and coal. Lorries and vans could be more nimble and were more suited to the retail and service economy to come.

Abandoned lines are everywhere, poking out of the grass. At the start of the 21st century we suddenly decided that they would make ideal linear parks: the High Line in New York, Paris's Promenade Plantée, the Goods Line in Sydney, the Folkestone Harbour Branch, the tracks threading silently through Tempelhof Airport in Berlin's newest park. It's odd that a kind of memento mori of the railways and their decline has become a way of making them cool again. And ironic, of course, that the popularity bestowed on these previously ignored and misunderstood arteries is irrelevant – they can never reopen as real railways because they are now popular parks.

In Britain one word was synonymous with the hollowing out of the railways: Beeching. His axe fell on rural branch lines around the country, robbing towns and villages and suburbs of their railways and stations. Portishead lost a striking new station in 1964 that was barely ten years old. The reinstatement of that line and that station will surely happen in the next decade but whether the station will be cheap 'n' cheerful? Well, we are deep into an austerity age.

Writing on their blog, Historic England quotes Steven Parissien, author of *The English Railway Station*: 'Richard Beeching was an amateur in the railway world, economically out of his depth and politically awkward. Britain's railways were thus disembowelled by a man who should not have been let near a railway, let alone the Ministry of Transport.'

We tend to compare cars to trains but it's really buses that were seen as replacements too, or, as we often say in the Anglo world, 'coaches' to denote longer travel that involves motion sickness, Tardis toilets that are impossible to use if the driver is not maintaining a steady 5mph in a straight line, cramped conditions and cricked necks. Coaches also summon up memories of school trips, for teachers would be mad to let a load of kids go on a train with their constantly opening and closing doors. Whenever you see a group of kids in their now ubiquitous high-vis stepping on and off Tube trains it's enough to give you a heart attack thinking about the chances of one getting left behind sans iPhone. The Netflix show *Sex Education* perfectly nailed the school coach trip to France, even down to its set design where everything on the hired coach was brown and orange – as any child of the 1980s will remember. A coach can be a sealed and managed experience, which is why teachers love it and restless passengers will hate it – no leg stretching save for at the services.

In some countries buses (or coaches) quickly usurped trains; in the United States where railways were dismantled en masse, and in Spain where they languished in an underfunded malaise for decades until the AVE revolution. In some nations people will actively encourage you to take a bus and say their trains suck: Latvia and Bosnia and Herzegovina come to mind as places where I've been warned off the rails and on to the roads. In recent times coach companies have upped their game with very cheap fares and interiors that are not quite as cosy as Grandma's house but still better than some ageing trains: Lux Express, RegioJet and FlixBus shook things up in Central Europe.

Conversely, in countries like Britain, the coach is really seen as being a total step down that exists solely for those on very tight budgets (isn't that everyone these days?) or travelling at weird times like on Christmas Day or to Stansted Airport at 3am. Bus stations have often reflected the fact that buses have been seen as a little seedy. Anyone who has issues with Deutsche Bahn's station infrastructure is probably someone who expects a little more from life and possibly has never had to endure the much worse barren wasteland of Berlin's Zentraler Omnibusbahnhof – an experience that, unsurprisingly, is documented in *We Children from Bahnhof Zoo*, where the Zoo train station is filled with pimps and prostitutes, while the bus station is even wilder, windier and if anything more scary. Prague's bus station is a car crash and many cities have the most rudimentary collection of shelters and

roofs purporting to be a bus station – unmanned, cold, lonely and as far from the glamour of travel as you can imagine. Some bus stations have found fame for their bizarre horror-film interiors, like the Port Authority Terminal in New York, final stopping point of waifs and strays and a big fixture in David Simon's *The Deuce*. Tel Aviv's compellingly crazy megastructure of ramps, malls, bomb shelters, soldiers and hobos asking for 20 shekels is one of the world's most bizarre bus stations. A very few bus stations have achieved legendary status – Building Design Partnership's restored Preston is probably the world's best; Derby's Art Deco masterwork was also something to behold. At least with a train you get a station – sometimes you have to wait for a Megabus on the street, leaning on a lamp post.

We oversimplify eras like we oversimplify people: the 70s was bell bottoms and Bowie; this person is a rogue and this one is an angel. We end up having shorthand. With places too: Berlin is Berghain, Monte Carlo is money, Birmingham is … concrete? So although the period from 1950 to the end of the century was indeed dominated by road building and cars, it was not entirely the end of trains. There was some flowering of new, innovative solutions – especially in high-speed intercity lines and urban metros.

Grand railway schemes were still being dreamed up around the world: Japan's Shinkansen, France's TGV (*Train à Grande Vitesse*), Rio's Metro. New stations were coming onstream, there was a desire to modernize the creaking Victorian infrastructure in Europe, and for those that had never got their railways or city metro systems in the developing world they wanted it. Some countries like Austria and Switzerland and Russia and India never gave up on their trains.

But the railways would have to be better. Japan's bullet trains and then Germany's ICE (Inter City Express) became world leaders. New stations like those in Kyoto and Kassel were built for the new high-speed lines. In Britain, the start of the rail revolution meant something special had to happen too – the APT (Advanced Passenger Train) story gets its own section later in this Introduction, as does the modernization of the West Coast Main Line, which gave Britain its first truly modern railway and beautiful stations like Coventry. And although the Euston Arch had been lost, the 1960s Euston Station looked clean and calm like an airport terminal before it got mucked about with in the later decades.

The new stations for the new towns at Harlow and Milton Keynes looked modern and were slightly quirky outliers in such car-led places. As train travel slowly began to increase again from the 1990s onwards, we needed to update so many stations, especially in London, and the likes of Nick Derbyshire and Alastair Lansley overhauled Liverpool Street. Derbyshire worked with Nicholas Grimshaw on Waterloo International. Farrells' London Bridge looked fantastic with its wood and lofty heights. Improvements to King's Cross and Paddington brought things up to standard. But it was St Pancras that became the showiest of all stations in the British capital – a real link between the present and the first railway golden age of York Station and Wemyss Bay in Scotland.

If the trains in rural areas suffered from a bad case of the axe in Britain, the USA and Argentina, then urban areas at least were spared – in some ways. Cars did kind of make sense in the countryside, even though rural towns that lost their stations would never do as well as those that retained them. And even if Americans have all but given up on trains, certainly British market towns are falling over themselves to get their station and their branch line back, with a new generation of lighter trains like the Parry People Mover or Vivarail's repurposed Tube Stock, which has had its problems but hopefully has a future, sometimes seen as the answer. More innovations will no doubt come as we see the Earth is on fire and realize that we need greener ways to get

around. The newly reopened stations in places like Kenilworth show the way to a new future.

But while all this was happening in the countryside the urban story was different. Heavy rail and freight rail declined, with some of the least-used stations being the ones with very limited services near industrial areas or in locations just outside of city centres like Ardwick or Bordesley. Old freight lines and terminals became things like the High Line.

The metro story is very different. These lines have thrived even through the car era, because even the most boneheaded politician or auto lobbyist recognized the need for mass transit in dense areas (except LA, ignored for years, and which is finally catching up). New York and London cannot commute to Wall Street and the City en masse in cars, so there needs to be massive-capacity public transport.

New York's Subway very obviously faced tough times though in the 20th century as the money ran out and the fear of crime increased. Vintage photos of *Warriors*-era Subway trains covered in graffiti are a stark contrast to today's clean, efficient system. A system which, of course, New Yorkers love to moan about and one that is very far from perfect and in need of a lot of TLC, but nevertheless can get you all over the city at any time of day and night, speedily and for just 30-odd bucks a week. Which, in the world's most expensive city, is about the only bargain you're going to get any more. Personally I could not be happier riding these rails in the dead of night, surrounded by the sleeping hobos and shift workers, seeing what the city is really like and experiencing the filth and the fury as J. G. Ballard and Jonathan Meades would encourage us to do, knowing I'd otherwise be dropping 100-odd bucks on an Uber from the Upper East Side to somewhere out in the middle of Bed-Stuy.

The removal of the elevated 'L' lines took away some of the drama of the stations, though you can still find those above the roofs of Brooklyn. And obviously Chicago has kept its 'L' stations too, which are quaint relics of how city transit was envisioned

before America sank its subways in the ground. If New York's Subway stations are rather like fast-food joints, Grand Central is the Michelin-starred *grande dame*. It speaks of an age when railways had the power and money, and getting a train on Metro-North like *The Nutmegger* is majestic. Tourists come just to marvel, stopping briefly to stare in awe. And once they're finished looking at iPhones in the Apple store they stare up at the ceiling.

London's Underground was built to connect the central terminal stations which were not central enough – by way of an aside here, it's worth noting how some stations are impossibly central within the city like Birmingham New Street, while the likes of Cambridge involve ridiculous walks. The newer Parkways and (in Europe) TGV stations are even further from the centre.

But having connected the end stations of the nation's railways, the Underground spread out into the suburbs. Its design and architecture are worthy of UNESCO status and the London Transport Museum and its shop showcase this incredible array of visual treats – from seat moquettes to wall maps, posters and trains. Mark Ovenden's books point out the sheer beauty of the maps and diagrams that different systems around the world use, many inspired by the simplified Harry Beck London map, which looks like a sort of circuit board.

London's Charles Holden stations in particular are enough to make you spit out your tea. The 1930s Piccadilly Line Extension stations like Southgate (which looks like it was inspired by a flying saucer and a spark plug), Arnos Grove, Oakwood and Cockfosters are brilliant suburban modernism. The canopy over the bus station at Newbury Park unites two foes and shows that both can have good architecture – it looks so clean and futuristic. And talking of futuristic, the more modern stations of the Jubilee Line Extension from the 1990s like West Ham, Westminster and North Greenwich have a cocaine swagger too, like a kind of Cool Britannia expressed in postmodern architecture.

Metros have flourished, with lauded new systems coming to Washington, DC and Bilbao and Prague and São Paulo. New lines and new stations have been added to almost every other metro and subway and sometimes they have looked great. Vienna's Metro is a super-clean and efficient exercise in doing the basics well – with a mix of the showy Art Nouveau Stadtbahn stations and the late 1970s red, white and orange stops that are just simple, clean and always there for you.

Trams, streetcars, light rail – whatever you want to call it, systems that sometimes run on rails on streets and sometimes on segregated rails like a train are coming back to cities too, from Dallas to Portland, Nottingham, Sheffield, Edinburgh, LA, Odense, AlUla in Saudi Arabia, Kiel, Caen, Doha, Coventry. Vienna, Melbourne and St Petersburg never gave up on their trams like London and Paris did. The appeal of these systems is obvious, blending the best of bus with train. Stations are often more like simple stops but that does not mean architects can't have fun with them, like J.MAYER.H's Europaplatz tram interchange in that most green of cities, Freiburg.

The explosion in city living and the rampant urbanization of the developing world will keep metros and subways doing their business, especially in Asia where there are always new projects on the table to get the congested supercities moving more easily. The opening of a metro in Brasilia was a totem in a way – that the city designed for the car had finally succumbed to the lure of the train.

Railways went through the same kind of three-act play as something like housing, at least in the UK. Dominated by horrendous private speculators at the outset, then essentially nationalized and seen as a public asset in the people's century, then privatized during the new capitalist wild west that has seen a once proud nation asset-stripped by the super-rich and enter a Venezuelan economic death spiral spurred on by these same hedge-fund elites, Russian backers, media barons and disgraceful politicians and their idiotic supporters. Social housing and the NHS were the supreme achievements of 20th-century Britain as the railways were the supreme achievement of the century before. Now? Everything has a price tag. The irony of course is that the British train companies are today owned by the state railways of countries who aren't run by (quite as) greedy idiots: Germany, Singapore, Hong Kong, France, the Netherlands. The US railway companies were all powerful. When Amtrak was nationalized something once proud became a thing of shame. It's funny how things change. They don't everywhere, though: France has an iron grip on its state-run railways and will always protect SNCF.

Will Britain ever renationalize? The British system, with its many companies and stupid amount of tickets, is a mess. Yet the trains are new and the system is expanding. It's a complex picture. There's no doubt though that worldwide people want to travel on cheap, comfortable, fast, reliable trains – especially with oil prices going through the roof. Germany's nine-euro ticket showed this. (Re)build the railways and they shall come. Even in the USA – if it's a good enough system. Not everyone wants to drive.

Trains have come back into fashion – even fashion itself has approved railways. Gucci holds launches on trains when previously labels would have embraced cars and planes. Francis Bourgeois scoots to launches and posts Instagram Reels. His enthusiasm riles some of the purist trainspotters but that sunniness shows what us train fans know. When he giggles as the *Sir Nigel Gresley* thunders by, we smile too.

But here's another thing – as someone who loves trains, planes and roads in different ways, am I some kind of freak? As with today's politics, apparently ne'er the twain shall meet. Green train fans tut at drivers and plane passengers, pedestrians and cyclists bicker, car drivers hate everyone but especially buses and cyclists, and they think railways are a joke. Everyone is stuck in their own lane, waging war with everything else. But the thing with railways is they can be all things to all people. Most car mad drivers will accept that the Elizabeth Line is a bobby-dazzler and the most Avios-addicted flyer will secretly relish the Eurostar.

However, there's a yawning chasm between the apparent reality and the sometimes gory situation on the ground: railways can be rubbish. I admit this as a 10/10 train fan. I wonder, though, when I read the endless 'joy of train travel' features in the British travel press whether all is what it seems. Some of these writers seem never to have taken a cross-border train before and are agog simply at the novelty of it all. Jon Worth was sent seemingly as a calmer voice on these matters, elucidating the horror of delays and cancellations that only those in the know will have repeatedly experienced at the border stations we all love to hate – Frankfurt (Oder), Děčín, Aachen. You haven't lived as a train traveller until you've spent four hours somewhere between Vienna and Prague at a station with no announcements in English, wondering what the hell is going on while sharing Marlboro Golds with Israeli backpackers in the sun.

Perhaps there is an over-romanticism of train travel that is not reflected on the ground. In these stories the writer always seems to be travelling in first class on an ICE or something, spending lunch in the restaurant car. Come to think of it, you can read one of these that I wrote for *The Independent* later on in this book. If you're unlucky enough to be rammed on a train that's picking up another cancelled train of people plus their luggage and the air con's off and the buffet has sold out of 7Days croissants and biscuits, then your perch in the corridor by the stinking toilets might not seem quite so suited to a broadsheet double spread.

But trains today are even challenging private jets and cars as prestige modes, just like in the Agatha Christie age. A society murder would look so slick, on the restored Belmond Orient Express or the luxury GoldenPass Express from Interlaken to Montreux.

There's a predictability about trains you don't get with roads. In theory. A bus timetable isn't worth the paper it's written on. Devotees of Google Maps or users of Uber will know the ETAs are pointless – you may as well shout out fake numbers like 'Twevelty!' in Mitchell & Webb's fake gameshow Numberwang. Roads and driving are full of open-ended possibilities – that's one way cars have always been sold, as agents of personal freedom. You have to wait for a train, you have to use a clock. Time was irrelevant before trains, then the Swiss railway clock became the apotheosis of time as a railway-sponsored notion in a railway obsessed nation. Railways by their nature are guided by tracks, by times, by stations and patterns.

It is no coincidence that neurodiverse trainspotters love these predictable worlds which are safer in some way than the chaotic outside world that tests them. Numbers, letters, patterns, times, timetables, organization, logistics – the railway is a machine. Aviation is like this. Its globalized, standardized systems in IT, ticketing, airport codes, booking, websites, marketing, branding are all ripped from the playbook the railways wrote and then kind of forgot about. If rail wants to take on low-cost airlines for international journeys it needs to play the airlines at this game again, essentially making it much easier to buy tickets and have the certainties that flying gives you. Flying is going to have a very big image problem soon (it probably does already) and railways could score an open goal.

And, as cars and roads become more closed in, more taxed, with more cameras and monitoring, more regulations, more blocked-off streets, then train travel becomes the freer option in a way when you look at shorter journeys too. Urban trains don't need timetables really – turn up and go, you can take your bike on them, you don't have to pay your road tax and parking fines.

It's the revenge of the nerds. The geeks who couldn't get the girls because they were out with a notebook collecting numbers are now getting numbers of a different kind, and they can't believe their luck. Trains, like their fans, were the losers of the transport world and now everyone loves them. Would this book have even been commissioned a few years ago? As with my previous delves into worlds like lidos and parks – two weird municipal undertakings that have made an unlikely comeback, just like the idiot who wrote books about them, I seem destined to tell the stories of the most boring stuff that's on its way back into fashion. And if you want to hear stories of boring stuff then slide into my DMs whenever you wish, because the boring stuff is what I'm into.

Look at how many times you see trains and subways and metros in 'American' movies. Hardly ever. It's always characters driving cars. It's notable that the two movies where you do see trains (both incidentally films Richard Linklater was involved with) are two of the best modern romances ever made – a template, if you will, for my own modest dreams of writing a low-budget romcom that resonates. *In Search of a Midnight Kiss* shows something I can't think of any other LA movie doing: characters taking the Red Line subway during the course of a date. It's a beautiful, wistful, wonderful love story. And in the rather better known *Before Sunrise*, Richard Linklater's characters meet on a train outside Vienna and walk that city's streets while they fall in love (they also jump on an iconic red Vienna tram). They could not have met over a petrol-station pastry at a service area – the train is intrinsic to everything about the story and the characters. Train passengers read books, daydream, eat long lunches. Car passengers listen to music and fidget. Railways tug at heartstrings. Watching a train depart is the memory of a long-distance love affair at university, the tears on Platform 7 at Leeds on a Sunday evening, seeing the other couples in a similar spot as one heads off to Bristol or Manchester or Newcastle. *Brief Encounter* and its setting at Carnforth Station are pure cinematic magic, pure suburban sorrow, pure truth about relationships, pure sadness at how the British keep calm and carry on in loveless marriages.

No brand in London or Berlin would ally itself with the car today, unless perhaps it is a softened and slightly inauthentic personal mobility entity that preaches green values and runs on peas. Flight shaming will, one assumes, only gather in momentum. Eco protesters are the tip of the arrow of opinion. Will we boycott airports and roads in ten years as we do milk and meat today?

How green are trains though? The ultimate answer in the war of being woke is simply to stay at home every day and eat cabbage you grow in your bedroom, with the heating off and visitors naturally unsettled when they come round. Do you want to live like this? Or do we see a value in travelling and meeting other humans, in experiencing places and events? If so, somehow you have to get there. And a unicycle won't always cut the mustard.

If we say trains are the answer, well, how much is that even true? Those who opposed HS2 in Britain argued that cutting down ancient oaks in the Chilterns for a new railway line was not helping the planet. The Riviera Maya Railway scheme in Mexico might cut car and plane journeys but it also looks like a hell of a lot of concrete and metal being dumped on a large area of jungle so a lot of foreign tourists can travel more speedily. Having spent a bit of time in the Yucatan one wonders if the area really needs any more American tourists. In Kenya and Goa, in France and Italy, new rail lines have been opposed. In China it sometimes looks like lines to such places as Lhasa have political dimensions beyond the apparent infrastructural additions.

What will tomorrow's stations and railways say about the way we view our trains? In Geoff Marshall's always entertaining videos, we see the new stations that are sometimes impressive, like Farringdon on the Elizabeth Line, and the ones in rural areas that are a little more meat and potatoes – they don't have the same grandeur as the Victorian edifices that celebrated the brand-new technology of the railways in not-so-subtle style. We can overcome small budgets for new stations by thinking imaginatively. Opening stations is good – and you can make them look cool without much money too. Let's be proud of the ones that do come back on stream.

The railway is one of mankind's supreme inventions. It got us from A to B when no one really took those journeys. And while there are thousands of futuristic inventions dedicated to a future of constant mobility, maybe this Victorian notion can be the real and less glamorous answer to our problems.

While I was in Central America finishing writing this book (no, I didn't get there by train), it was announced that El Salvador is building two new lines and Guatemala is to reactivate its dormant railway. Dhaka opened its new subway, Britain's HS2 will be coming in some form or another, Maryland's Purple Line is on track, Bogota's subway is coming, the China to Nepal line is being built, Rail Baltica will link Tallinn to Riga, Kaunas and Warsaw, Thailand is opening new high-speed lines, Indonesia too – like Jakarta to Bandung. The investment and optimism are endless. The infrastructure makes it: without the Channel Tunnel you couldn't have quick Eurostar journeys from London to Brussels and Paris. The Fehmarn Belt tunnel under the Baltic will make it a cinch to go from Copenhagen to Hamburg and Berlin by train. It's time to choo-choo-choose rail. And to make sure that each new station sings about the heritage of the mechanism and the power of its future.

Today, as never before since the mid-1800s, we are all Michael Portillo wearing salmon trousers and a mauve jacket in the BBC TV smash *Great Railway Journeys*, embarking on journeys for work or fun and seeing the pleasure in riding the rails and being among the buildings that define the lines and the second age of the train.

UK

KING'S CROSS
London

Living in the midst of the changes around King's Cross over the years gave me a strangely personal take on this station and the area around it. It was – as for many northerners too I suppose – the first place I set foot in London. I remember the shabby old hotels and the smoky station, then years of boarded-up building works and weekend cancellations until finally the extravagant new waiting hall, by McAslan and Stirling Prize-nominated, opened next to the station. It's not perfect, but then what is in life? The one-way systems, access routes and circulation are a bit dodgy – trying to find a lost aunt from Sunderland can be tricky. But it's got a charm that has rippled out around it too. The side streets I watched change seismically when I lived on York Way from 2008 to 2011 have become home to people and businesses, the clubs like The Cross left and the luxury shops of Coal Drop Yards came. And then Google decided to build an HQ next door in what was once one of London's worst areas. Strange how things change. Obviously it's all a ruse to make money from property because what isn't in Britain today? But the station is a place that people mostly enjoy – even if the up-and-over escalator to the platforms seems beyond most passengers' comprehensions as they stare at it like a mongoose trying to solve a Rubik's Cube – then give up and take the ground-level route instead.

Entrance ⬅ 🚉 No entry ⛔

DOCKLANDS
LIGHT RAILWAY

London

Put your hand up if you don't rush for the front seat on a DLR train. And if not – why, for heaven's sake? Trains are supposed to be fun. That's why we make the choice to go and ride on steam railways and visit railway museums when we could be in bed. The automated DLR means you can (mostly) grab that front pew and get a great view of the engineering and architecture that makes up the system in east London's Docklands. The vintage 1980s stations of the original incarnation are hard to spot but Devons Road remains deliberately preserved in aspic, with its blue and red colour scheme propelling you back to the Big Bang era when the derelict Docklands were to be the site of a ton of postmodern developments put up by coked-up developers, with the elevated railway linking them all. The overhead tracks make the trains much more visible and the stations in the sky like South Quay (whose new iteration perched above the water reminds me of a Hamburg Hochbahn station like Baumwall) are more fun than being down in the bowels of the ground. The big interchange at Canary Wharf is a pomo edifice, which even features Spanish solution platforms, where the train doors open on both sides at the same time – another kid-friendly set piece. In fact, come to think of it, the whole DLR feels like a big toy train set.

ELIZABETH LINE

London

It took longer to finish the Elizabeth Line than it does to finish the Christmas Day washing up. And it came with even more squabbles. It feels like (despite the delays) a Britain doing things right. It's hard to fault the ambition and the size and space of the stations. It doesn't feel like a country falling apart – but then it was supposed to be there years and years ago, before Brexit and the wheels coming off. The platforms at Farringdon and Liverpool Street stretch between two Underground stations, and walking the length of them keeps your Fitbit happy. The white colour scheme feels fresh and modern and, combined with the platform-edge doors, it's pure *Star Wars* space-age camp. Londoners couldn't believe that travelling could be so comfortable – our Underground is so old and clattery, this feels like the real deal. It's how new metro lines in developing cities feel. Knitting regional routes out to Shenfield, Abbey Wood, Reading and Heathrow makes the south-east's rail system so much more efficient. Though some of us still like to think of it as Crossrail, the project name for a decade.

Simon Calder

on the highs and lows of riding the rails

*Simon is one of Britain's foremost and most recognizable
travel and transport journalists. simoncalder.co.uk*

Tell us briefly why you like train travel.
I love travel, and for journeys that I can't
sensibly walk or cycle, rail is the optimum
mode of transport: safe, often fast, usually
convivial, sometimes beautiful.

**Simon, you are the expert – what
are your feelings on stations you've
visited on your travels?**
Hated: almost anywhere in the USA. Sadly,
a nation built by the railroad has turned
its back on trains. In Detroit, for example, I
imagined that the Amtrak terminal would
be a grand departure point. It turned out
to be an ungainly waiting room adjacent
to a windswept platform. This pattern is
repeated at dozens – possibly hundreds –
of other stations.

**We're looking at modern railways.
Which modern stations in the UK
do you love and loathe?**

From Plymouth to Taunton to Oxford to
Birmingham New Street to Derby to Leeds,
the post-war reconstruction of railway
stations has mostly been aesthetically
catastrophic. In London, St Pancras, King's
Cross, Marylebone and Paddington show
how stations can be successfully modernized.
Post-war London Bridge and Glasgow
Queen Street were awful, and the 21st-
century versions are much improved.

**Any future rail projects around
the world you're excited about?**
The permanent monthly 49-euro ticket in
Germany is the most exciting development.

Any funny stories from days on the rails in foreign climes?

The journey from Parma in Italy to the lovely though little-known town of Sarzana looked simple on paper (and on the excellent Trenitalia app). From Parma (where, quaintly, all visitors spending a euro visiting the loo on Platform 1 are given a handwritten receipt) the train would thread through the mountains to Pontremoli – a town whose name means 'trembling bridge' – and, six minutes later, a connecting service would depart for Sarzana and Florence. What could possibly go wrong? Well, the train left late and fell further behind schedule. A crackly public address announcement mentioned 'Firenze'. I asked a fellow passenger to decipher, expecting her to say:

'They won't hold the Florence train so we have to wait an hour or two for the next one.' Amazingly, she said instead: 'This train will follow the first one all the way to Florence. All you have to do is stay on board and you will get to your destination perhaps 15 or 20 minutes late.' And so it proved. A miracle on the railway.

If you were made Transport Minister tomorrow in the UK, what would you immediately do to the trains?

Reform ticketing. Single-leg pricing. Many prices will fall but some will rise, and a bold government would allow this to happen.

ST PANCRAS

London

Getting dumped not once but twice at Waterloo International did not enamour me to Nicholas Grimshaw's snaking structure for the original Eurostar, which today has been reborn as domestic platforms for Kent-bound trains, despite it looking swanky. St Pancras could surely only be an improvement (well, I haven't been dumped there – yet) and the verdict was quickly in: it heralded a new railway age in Britain. Many of the other new stations we've built since the Millennium have been cheap and not always cheerful – Leeds is a bit of a car crash and Coventry has erased the good work of the 1960s. St Pancras was a corker complete with the Champagne Bar and art by Tracey Emin that mixes cool with classy. The restoration would have made John Betjeman proud – he saved it from demolition and his lovely statue is given pride of place. The Spice Girls sang on the stairs of the hotel where my friends later got married and from the front you get a great view of the reimagined Camden Town Hall Annex, now a Standard Hotel. The upper level is quiet, the lower one rings out with pianos playing and is a proper gateway to Belgium and France, as Blackfriars and Victoria were in the boat train days. Now just to rejoin the EU and enter the Schengen Zone and everything will be fine.

METRO

Tyne & Wear

The only weakness in the BBC's bravura moustache-fest *Our Friends in the North*, which tells the story of the 20th century in spellbinding fashion, is that there isn't a storyline about the Metro. It can trace its ambitions back to T. Dan Smith's Newcastle of the 1960s, where the attempt was to build Brasilia on the Tyne. This gutsy belief in what could be achieved in a proud regional capital filtered down to the Metro project of the late 1970s and 1980s. It took local British Rail lines and added extensions and an underground loop through Newcastle's city centre. The automated trains meant you could sit at the front and pretend you were driving. The new underground Haymarket and Central Stations had a futuristic feel (Haymarket's smoked-brown glass drum was replaced with a bigger glass pod entrance in 2009). The graphics and logos look very much of their time and are by Margaret Calvert: the 'M' logo and the 'Metro' lettering are instantly recognizable and the system gave Tyne & Wear's citizens a way to get around that differed sharply from how Smith saw the car as being the future.

Signs of the Time

(from *The Independent*), UK

They are icons of the everyday, and arguably one of Britain's greatest 20th-century design achievements, and yet they rarely get the acknowledgement they deserve. But in 2024, the British Rail logo (designed by Gerry Barney), along with the whole signage scheme that once graced every British station, turns 60 years old.

It seems that as we rediscover the joys of state-funded architecture from the mid-20th century – the pleasures of tower blocks et al. – it is only fitting that we should pay homage to these other symbols of public sector optimism.

In 1964, Britain was a confident country driven by a progressive mentality rather than the make-do-and-mend ethos of governments today. New signs and designs for our roads and railways were meant to underline a future that would be fast and functional. And, in a studio in Knightsbridge, central London, fresh from designing signs for the new airport at Gatwick, graphic designers Jock Kinneir and Margaret Calvert were creating the standard layout for the signs that would be the visual language of the new bridges, bypasses and motorways snaking across a Britain in thrall to technology and the car.

Kinneir set out to make signage that would be legible even from the seat of a car shooting past at 70mph. One

Printed Publicity
**Symbol and logotype
in colour for rail publicity**

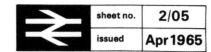

a. Symbol and logotype in BR Publicity Red

b. Symbol in **BR Publicity Red** with logotype in
black

c. Symbol and logotype within ruled rectangles
all in **BR Publicity Red**

d. Symbol and logotype in BR Publicity Red
within ruled rectangles in black

e. Symbol in BR Publicity Red with logotype in
black within ruled rectangles in black

The British Rail *Corporate Identity Manual*, symbol and logotype in colour for rail publicity, April 1965.

Rail alphabet
Combined sheet - lowercase

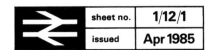

sheet no.	**1/12/1**
issued	**Apr 1985**

This sheet must be used for all lettering applications in preference to sheets 1/11 and 1/12

The British Rail *Corporate Identity Manual*, Rail Alphabet combined sheet – lowercase, April 1985.

trick was to use upper and lowercase letters rather than all capitals, plus different background colours: blue on motorways, green on A-roads. Meanwhile, Calvert, who was behind the various pictograms, wanted the signs to be friendly, and the characters in them to be warmly human, bringing life to our pavements and junctions.

The signs are masterpieces. But they also nag us. They point us in the right direction yet they warn us not to stray. They are poignant symbols of a country that loves rules yet moans about the people who make and enforce them.

They have also suffused our culture: fashion designer Anya Hindmarch's Autumn/Winter collection in 2015 featured bags, sweaters and the like emblazoned with signage she saw on the M25; musician Jimmy Cauty of the KLF used the signs more satirically in his 'model village' at Banksy's Dismaland;

the film-maker Patrick Keiller shoots roundabout signs at length and zooms in on the lichens that live on them in his bravura *Robinson* films about a Britain on the brink; and children of the 90s may remember the infamously over-hyped band Gay Dad, and their appropriation of the pedestrian-crossing man on posters that appeared everywhere and were enigmatically devoid of text.

'I think a lot of these pictograms drawn by Margaret are so well-crafted and elegant that they've become part of the British landscape, whether the digging man, or the schoolchildren ... or the cattle [warning] sign in which Margaret referenced a relative's cow called Patience!' jokes Patrick Murphy. The girl in the schoolchildren crossing sign? Calvert based her drawing on a photo of herself as a child, immortalizing herself in every British town and village.

As well as creating a new typeface, Transport, which was used on all road signs, Kinneir and Calvert also dreamt up one called Rail Alphabet for use on railway signs in the same year. These signs were similarly clean, crisp and elegant – in 1965 British Rail was building brutalist signal boxes and modernist stations, while replacing steam engines with diesel, and its graphic identity also had to look to the future.

That year British Railways was rebranded as British Rail and also got a new logo – the double arrow and railway lines, which even today is used as a symbol for a train station, although BR has bitten the dust. It's an instant signifier that says, 'This is where you catch a train.'

'Like the motorway signs, Gerry Barney's BR symbol is important because it still works,' says Mark Sinclair, author of *TM: The Untold Story Behind 29 Classic Logos*, in which it features. He says the typeface and logo 'were applied to every part of the railway system – from rolling stock to stations and offices, signposts, posters and publicity material, uniforms and cutlery. Even the shortening of British Railways to British Rail evoked a sense of streamlining and modernization.'

As the 20th century faded, and the privatization of our rail network took root, graphic design on railway platforms has turned into a visual car crash of orange and purple, green and yellow, perpetrated by all our dysfunctional rail operators. Every company has its own designs today: most of them are terrible. The unified BR design was simple, clear and continuous, but, like BR itself, that's all gone. Still, at least Kinneir and Calvert's road signs are still going strong.

Printed Publicity
**British Rail Catering
Packaging examples**

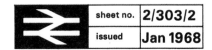

	sheet no.	**2/303/2**
	issued	**Jan 1968**

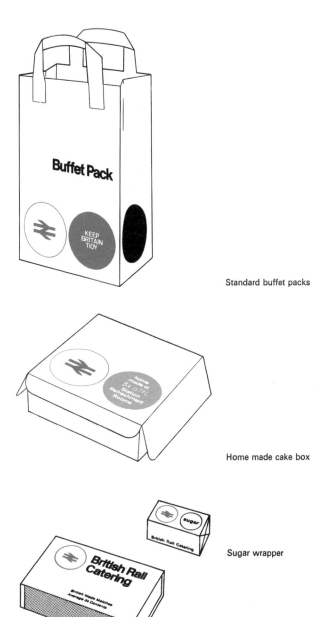

Standard buffet packs

Home made cake box

Sugar wrapper

Match box

The British Rail *Corporate Identity Manual*, British Rail Catering Packaging examples, January 1968.

LONDON
BRIDGE

London

London Bridge Station has been rightly
acclaimed for its stylish redevelopment of
what was a problematic bottleneck with
both terminating and through-running trains
to south-east London and Kent. The high
platforms are nicely poised and the use of
wood contrasts with the existing brick arches.
The Shard towers over the place and it all
feels like a mix of old London and a more
property-focused future. Older readers might
remember getting drunk in the arches next to
and under the station – a recurring theme in
the UK where many night clubs made use of
this space, for instance Ministry of Sound here,
Corsica Studios nearby and the Warehouse
Project in Manchester.

QUEEN STREET

Glasgow

Queen Street has never had the grandeur of the later Glasgow Central, which felt more like a big city terminus. It also has that chippy outside, with a picture of Justin Bieber in the window reminding us of when he went for a fish supper there once. However, the 2017–21 Queen Street refurbishment has given the station back some of the glamour it was lacking. The biggest change is the removal of a 1960s tower block and the opening up of the front and the new façade, which makes it feel more important and certainly makes it more visible. From the Greggs across George Square where you'll be stocking up on Scotch pies, bridies and cream buns for your journey to Mallaig or Aberdeen or Perth, you can now see the station with its golden top, and inside there's more room to breathe.

THE APT SAGA

The 1976 High Speed Rail (InterCity 125) looked glorious with its handsome yellow nose designed by Sir Kenneth Grange, and the high-speed train remains in service in England and Scotland to this day. It was even exported to Australia. Britain's attempt at a new higher-speed train for the 1980s is the stuff of legend: a torrid tale, essentially ruined – like many a marriage, friendship and office Christmas party – by booze. On a test run journalists got sick not because of the tilting, which we tolerate on the Italian-built Pendolinos that now ply the route, but because of the massive amounts of Brew XI and Dry Sack served. If only British Rail had stuck with the Advanced Passenger Train the railways would have been revolutionized. Built for the twisty tracks of the West Coast Main Line, the 1970s trains would have complemented the 1960s stations on the line and Britain's modernist railway would have been a cracker. Today an original APT prototype sits forlornly at Crewe in the railway museum reminding us of that ambitious era – even the interiors (tartan in homage to the end of the line in Glasgow) and Travellers Fare food menus were designed to be cool and modern. Modern? You bet. It even had a film featuring BBC *Blue Peter*'s Peter Purves taking a trip to Glasgow.

HACKNEY WICK STATION

London

It's worth picking out Hackney Wick because so many other new British stations on a small scale already look so dire and decrepit as a result of being done quickly and on the cheap. This is not. The brazen use of raw concrete and big, industrial spaces feels right at home in this area of east London, which used to be home to foul factories and is now ground zero for furiously Instagramming hipsters. Coloured glass and aluminium also emphasize the sheer creativity and care that has gone into this overground station. Not a cookie cutter in site. Just a pity it's also a kind of vessel for the real-estate development and property greed that goes on nearby.

Dan Elkan

on connecting the rails to the slopes

Dan Elkan is founder of Snowcarbon. snowcarbon.co.uk

Tell us about your idea of trains to the slopes

Some friends invited me on a ski holiday. I knew nothing about skiing – it was just something that other people did. So I thought I'd give it a go. I turned up at Gatwick Airport at 5am on a Saturday morning, as I'd been instructed to do. We were headed for Andorra. There were thousands of people, shuffling around, looking miserable, even though they were supposed to be about to go on holiday. For the next 11 hours it was airport queues, security, a cramped flight, more queues and a long, cramped transfer. I couldn't believe how a short flight on paper could translate to extensive hours of transport misery in reality. We eventually got there. And the skiing made it all worth it. I thought the laborious journey to Andorra had been a one-off. But the next ski trip, to Italy, the

journey repeated itself. It seemed a bit ridiculous that so many people go through this polluting journey to get to pristine nature, too. This time, while slumped against the window of the transfer coach as we neared the resort of Sauze d'Oulx I noticed something glittering in the sunshine below. It turned out to be a railway track. And it made me wonder whether we could have come all the way from the UK by train, instead.

Back in the UK I dug out an old European rail timetable from my parents' attic – a relic of a student Interrail trip years before. Incredibly, London to Oulx required only two trains – one a direct TGV from Paris – and, door-to-door, was almost as quick as flying. How many other resorts could be reached easily by train? No one seemed to know, so I started researching. I got a map of Europe and began ploughing through the timetable, plotting possible routes. It was like putting

together a jigsaw puzzle where you didn't know what the pieces looked like, but just knew the final picture would be worth it. And the more I searched, the more I discovered. Plenty of resorts in France, Switzerland, Austria, Italy – even Andorra – could be reached by daytime or overnight train. I persuaded my skiing friends to let me plan our next trip by train. It was a gamble. What if the journey didn't work out as planned? It would be my fault. Yet there was no way I was going to be herded through airports for the rest of my skiing days without at least giving the train a go. The moment the Eurostar slipped quietly out of Waterloo, my fears melted away. Our holiday had already begun. There was no way of going back to flying, and I kept organizing ski holidays by train. It would be amazing to see how the journey made a difference, to see friendships forming en route because on the train people feel like they are already on holiday, on an adventure together.

A few years later, when I started working as a journalist, I wrote a travel feature for *The Guardian* about how to reach ski resorts by train. Soon I was writing articles like this two or three times a season, for *Ski+board*, the *Daily Mail*, *The Observer*, *Snowboard* and others.

And tell us how you are doing it now?

It's really difficult to get train operators to do things differently. In 2016, SNCF decided to axe most of its sleeper train routes. I campaigned to try to persuade it not to, and made a film about teddy bears travelling by sleeper train all the way to the French Alps. Neither I, nor the teddies, were successful at the time. However, in 2026 France are bringing ten sleeper train routes back again. So progress is being made.

The problem is that train operators do things without consulting or including the industries they serve.

Why do you love night trains and why are they coming back?

Night trains are a brilliant – and exciting – way of using your travel time. They allow you to go long distances while lying flat on your back, asleep. It's the equivalent of a magic carpet, in effect. There's a romance about them and they can be great fun. Some of the ones to the slopes even have disco carriages in them.

Why are trains so great – in your opinion?

Train travel means quality time – at a fraction of the environmental cost of flying or driving. It's quality chunks of time. I get more done on trains than I do working from home, and with scenery gliding by you feel like you are killing two birds with one stone. I find that train journeys can be wonderful sources of serendipity: you can end up in interesting conversations with strangers. You might meet the love of your life or just make a friend – for the journey or for life. I even joined the 'Metre High Club' en route to a ski resort, after we met in the disco carriage of a Dutch train to Austria.

Feeling positive about rail today?

If feels like so many things do with rail are decisions that must have been made by consultants with spreadsheets who know nothing about the real value of travelling well. Look at the Thameslink trains that were introduced a few years ago. Second class is effectively a cattle truck. None of the seats in second class have tables. All of the seats in first class do. The train companies have built these to try to maximize capacity, but they do so at the expense of a quality journey. Table seats don't even decrease capacity – and they transform the way you can use the time. The process of buying a ticket has got easier, but harder. Easier because you can do it online very quickly. Harder because there are a whole range of more

flexible tickets that you miss out on this way. I once tried to organize a trip to Wales for a bunch of friends at short notice. We nearly abandoned the trip because, looking online, all the fares from London to Hereford were advance tickets at about £60 each way, and the prices were creeping up as we were trying to coordinate which train everyone could get.

More out of curiosity than hope, I wondered whether there might be a flexible ticket that we didn't know about. I phoned up National Rail Enquiries and asked: yes, there was – a walk-on fare, which excluded the very fastest trains, which we could just turn up at the station and book before boarding. And it cost £27 return. This was a game-changer, and it meant our trip could go ahead. Looking online, we would never have found it.

Any new stations you like in the UK or abroad?

Cluses, in the Haute-Savoie, has been rebuilt with a huge lift-assisted walkway. No need to haul your luggage up and down the stairs. And there's a great view from the bridge, too.

NEW STREET
SIGNAL BOX

Birmingham

This brutalist behemoth stood proud next to
Birmingham's main station, controlling the
thousands of trains trundling in and out every
day. The box is part of the 1960s modernization
of Britain's West Coast Main Line from London
to Liverpool, Manchester and Glasgow, where
Victorian rail infrastructure was mercilessly
trashed in an attempt to build a better, more
efficient railway for the new age – at the
same time that most transport spending was
heading towards motorways and airports.
Some other gems from the era of the West
Coast Main Line upgrade were London Euston
with its airy main hall, Manchester Oxford
Road, more brutalism at Stafford, plus the
incredible lightness and space of Coventry
Station. Sadly, Coventry has recently been
mucked about with and Euston was packed
with tat, its minimalism compromised just as
Stansted Airport would be so crassly a few
years later. But of course sacrifices were made,
like the loss of the Euston Arch when the old
Euston was demolished – raising questions
about how far progress should be going. A lot
of the problems stemmed from air rights – the
new idea that railway companies could make
money allowing skyscrapers to be built over
tracks and stations – this is why New Street
ended up so dark with a shopping centre
on top.

EUROPE

ART TRAM

Düsseldorf, Germany

Ads are everywhere and spoil the spaces we inhabit. It's like the uncle you don't want at any family party but who always comes, burping and cursing and making a show of himself while he quotes Jordan Peterson. He has not been invited to Düsseldorf. The Wehrhahn pre-Metro tram line funnels Düsseldorf's trams through underground tracks as is common here and in next-door neighbour Cologne, and through six stations over 3km (1¾ miles) of track that have no ads – and art instead. There's sound art in one – unsettling noises as you travel up the escalators (Ralf Brög); jagged patterns in the floor at another station (Heike Klussmann); a picture of a planet (Thomas Stricker); clashes of colours and lights (Ursula Damm); and red text (Enne Haehnle). It even has its own website and seems apt in the city famous for art and its big-bucks art fair.

The Joy of Interrail
(from *The Independent*), Europe

Interrailing should be a compulsory teenage rite of passage – no wonder various European countries have given out free passes to 18-year-olds. What better way to protect this beautiful, fragile union than by showing the next generation what they have in common with each other and how many hi-jinks they can get up to in neighbouring European countries?

It was my first taste of independent travel too – many summers ago, though it seems like yesterday. Back then it was a Karrimor loaded with band T-shirts, Lonely Planet *Europe on a Shoestring* and change for telephone boxes. I first interrailed in 2000 but decided to repeat the feat as an adult in 2017. This time, instead of sleeping cars, hostels and that tangy scent of socks, there were nice hotels and the scent of understated luxury. Three's 'Feel At Home' free roaming contract and my iPhone brought the whole experience into the 21st century, and meant home was only the touch of a button away.

It was a cultural whip-round the first time, but it was also a piss-up – getting out of your tree being the *sine qua non* of teenage travelling – that resulted in lost cash cards, nearly getting into fights on night trains and passing out on

Travellers arriving at Berlin Central Station (Berlin Hauptbahnof).

a Positano beach. And I met so many people – this was social networking *avant la lettre*, coming across fellow flâneurs from Australia, Canada and Finland, and making firm friends, if not for life then at least for a night.

Interrailing as an adult was more relaxed and even more cultured, with less boozing and earlier mornings. I sped through Rotterdam's Docklands on a water taxi, climbed all over Tomás Saraceno's incredible spider-web netting art installation five floors above the ground of Düsseldorf's Modern Art Gallery, had a preview of some of the exhibits at Kassel's famous art festival, Documenta, saw Eileen Gray furniture at Munich's Design Museum, drank at Wes Anderson's Bar Luce in Milan's Fondazione Prada, and explored New

Belgrade's brutalist architecture.

The food was better this time around too. Back in 2000 I had inadvertently explored the premise 'How can a human function on pizza alone for three weeks?' shortly after enduring the very worst meal of my entire life (do not ever accidentally order the minced heart and lung soup at Wörgl station buffet). This time I ate mushroom arancini with a vegetable mayonnaise in an old swimming pool in Rotterdam and fresh white asparagus at the BMW Welt's restaurant. Even the train food was good – on Deutsche Bahn's ICE I chowed down on lamb kofta with yoghurt and mashed carrots in the Bordrestaurant.

Full disclosure: I'm a bit of a trainspotter, but you don't need to be to enjoy Interrailing. It lets you see and experience a million things, and meet countless people along the way (even without the social lubricant of a bottle of ouzo). Interrailing is like an all-you-can-eat buffet of travel. With a ticket allowing 15 days of train journeys in a month, you can indulge like mad, stop anywhere, see anything. It's also about the random encounters: this time there was Natalie, the tipsy Teutonic tea lady who handed out biscuits on the Kassel–Munich express, and Tomi, the shifty journeyman who translated for me, winked his way around several conductors (I don't think he had a ticket) and helped us both not get stranded in the backwoods of Slovenia after a delay threatened a missed connection. He then promptly got dragged off the train by police when we entered Croatia; I wonder what became of him? Tomi, if you're reading this – please send me a postcard.

The best thing about Interrail is the flexibility. You can travel across Europe from Bodø to Badajoz, from Irun to Istanbul. My route traced a vaguely southbound arc from Holland to Serbia. At Belgrade I was having so much fun I decided to keep on going, looping back via Le Corbusier's Notre Dame chapel at Ronchamp to Paris, where my reward was a chance to unwind at Le Roch Hotel & Spa near to the Tuileries Garden, with gorgeous interiors by Sarah Lavoine. The next day I caught the Eurostar home, full of stories to tell. Staying on your train when you're supposed to get off is a small

Train carriage with a woodland view.

revolutionary act and from these seeds grows a belief that you can do anything and go anywhere.

It's also incredibly scenic. With a first-class pass you can sit in Swiss Railways' panorama coaches that snake through the Alps. From the windows of Serbian trains you can watch storks gliding over Balkan fields. On some German ICEs you can perch at the front and watch the driver and the rails flash by while bingeing on Spotify's 90s Emo playlists because the Wi-Fi is free. It's childish fun. And this is really the nub of Interrailing – whether you're 20, 40 or 60 you'll feel young and excited. Riding the rails is a timeless treat, a special sort of escapism on an increasingly crazy continent.

METRO AND HLAVNÍ NÁDRAŽÍ

Prague, Czech Republic

In many ways an archetypal Eastern Bloc metro system as Soviet as queues, boredom and bad hair days – Prague has its three lines in yellow, green and red (plus later additions). Nevertheless, Prague's 1974 system and stations have a special quality. The icon of the Metro is the walls of the stations on the initial section with their repetitive circular detailing, which makes you feel like a chocolate inside a wrapper, or a tuna stuck in a tin or a Lego brick on a bad trip. The Metro's focus is the Hlavní Nádraží, which is a real enigma. In many ways as hateful as a politician on the take, perhaps it does have a redeeming feature, providing dry, warm waiting space and retail. But by putting a motorway on its roof and trying to subvert and ignore the handsome old main station behind it, it's not a lesson in urban planning we'd go for today. At least they didn't demolish the old station.

ATOCHA

Madrid, Spain

Rafael Moneo's bonkers idea of closing the old Atocha train hall and installing a forest is even more inspired than it seemed in 1992. When you walk inside and discover this strange garden with its pools and birds in addition to the tall canopy of trees it really is like walking into a different world, and it fulfils the aim of reigniting the magic of travel in general and trains in particular. Those trains are now out the back in a newer extension, a bit like St Pancras too, I suppose. It also succeeds today as a symbol in an era when the railways are hard at it promoting themselves as a green alternative to airports. Airports were where the architectural elite used to really reside in the 20th century, each wanting to create a vision of the future that would often later become soiled by the unwanted addition of a pub. So Atocha, the first part of the AVE high-speed network stretching to Seville and now all around Spain, is worth lingering in.

HAUPT-BAHNHOF

Berlin, Germany

As we all know, Berlin was divided for the second half of the 20th century, and so in the 1990s the most important job of all was connecting up the parts of the city that had not functioned as one whole. The answer in the case of the railways was centralizing all long-distance services in one place. Previously western services ran into Zoo and eastern services into Ostbahnhof. Both of them are pleasing, plain, modern stations and there's something a little ghostly about both today as so much of their traffic was taken away and plonked in the Hauptbahnhof, itself on the site of an older station – the Lehrter Bahnhof, back when Berlin had a dozen terminal stations like Anhalter, Hamburger and Görlitzer, with routes radiating out across Prussia and its empire. Today's HBF is a place I seem to always be in, but I never tire of the 3D world you inhabit here, with the S-Bahn trains flying up high over your head and the ICEs down on the lower platforms, and now the new U5 connection too, with an additional north–south S-Bahn service also arriving. The station is a peach but the northern entrance towards Moabit is a spatial disaster area and needs to be tidied up, with roads and bike lanes and scrappy tarmac spoiling the experience of arrival.

Jon Worth

On European cross-border trains

Jon Worth tweets about cross-border European train travel
@jonworth from his Berlin base. jonworth.eu

Tell us about your personal experience of travelling Europe by train, Jon – the highs and lows.

For years I have been criss-crossing Europe by train for work – I'm self-employed and based in Berlin, and have clients in Copenhagen, Geneva, Maastricht, Brussels, Bruges, and occasionally work takes me even further afield. And I try to avoid flying, so that means relying on the train. So I have perfected very long-distance train travel for work purposes – coming to terms with the headaches of timetables and tickets that are often complex on international routes.

It's out of that personal experience that my determination to improve railways in Europe emerges – being able to work Europe-wide should be possible for more people.

But there is another side to it as well – when it works well travelling by train is a joy. There are classic wonderful routes I have taken – Bergen–Oslo, Bar–Belgrade, or the old line along the Rhine. Sat in the dining car on the train from Warsaw or Prague to Berlin on a summer evening is superb. And there are hidden gems – like pretty much any line in Slovenia, or the night trains from northern Finland to Helsinki.

But like any rail traveller I have had my fair share of nightmare experiences too – most recently huge delays crossing Poland, and insanely hot trains crossing Romania without air conditioning. And there are some railways in Europe that make me sad – notably Latvia, Croatia and Romania, where the basics do not work any more.

And tell us how you're trying to get better cross-border services. Now I've taken a lot of international trains in Europe, as have you, Jon – what are the main problems and any quick fixes from your end?

When you cross a border on a train in Europe everything gets worse or gets harder. Timetables are thinner. Getting tickets is harder. Working out if your train will run on time – if it started in another country – is often impossible. And there are dozens of cross-border railway lines in Europe that have either fallen into disrepair or are freight only.

Addressing some of these problems has been my main demand in the #CrossBorderRail project. From among the 95 internal borders of the EU I crossed in 2022, I drew up a Top 20 projects for the European Union – places where international railway services could be improved or restored quickly and easily. In many places it is as simple as running a train a few kilometres further to the first station after the border, rather than ending the service before the border, or making sure timetables at border stations are coordinated.

I hear all the time from the railway industry that investment in new lines is *the* solution for international rail, but I am not sure. In many parts of Europe the infrastructure is solid, but the service offered is not.

And as these are cross-border, Europe-wide problems, then the European Union needs to step up to solve them.

Why do you love night trains and why are they coming back?

I think 'love' is overdoing it a bit! Sure, there are wonderful overnight trips you can take, and what's not to like when waking up to the sunrise over the Mediterranean or snow on the Alps out of the window? But above all I essentially see night trains as something useful. Most people will not spend more than six hours in the daytime on a train, but they might overnight (indeed, studies show there is untapped potential for night trains in Europe – at least a few dozen more routes would be possible). You also save the cost of a night in a hotel. That, and a certain reminiscence for travel of the past, explains some of the current attention to night trains.

However, the picture is not altogether a rosy one. Only Austrian railways ÖBB has made any major investment in new night trains, and they cannot solve the lack of night trains on their own. The big railway companies – notably SNCF and Deutsche Bahn – have made little or no steps towards establishing new night train services. So my fear is that despite the attention, even hype, about night trains, they are likely to remain a niche service.

How can we make trains as appealing as low-cost airlines?

It might sound like an odd answer, but we need to first start with the user experience on trains. Make trains easier and more pleasurable to use. The trains that *are* like that already – in Switzerland and in Austria, for example – are generally also heavily used. Also, many trains on popular routes can be [fully] booked months ahead in summertime – so there we need more capacity. Longer trains, and more trains.

Then we come to the price. Take the Thalys trains that link Amsterdam, Köln and Brussels with Paris, for example. The cost per kilometre is horribly expensive, but at peak hours the trains are all full. Reducing the ticket price here is not going to get more people on the trains - because there is simply not enough capacity to accommodate all of them! Running slower and cheaper trains on underused infrastructure, so as to appeal to different parts of society - in the way FlixTrain operates in Germany - is interesting in this regard.

Tell us about any post-1945 stations and lines and trains you really enjoy?

The Tito-era Belgrade-Bar railway is a particular favourite - not least as the scenery is stunning, and the engineering quite a marvel as well. In the modern era I like Utrecht Centraal and Wien HBF very much; these both work impeccably well as railway stations, in a way my local station - Berlin HBF - does not. It looks nice, but the more you use it the more frustrating it is! Recent decades have seen the era of high-speed rail in Europe, and two lines stand out. The Florence-Rome Direttissima dates from the 1970s and started the high-speed trend - and is still the backbone of Italy's railway - and Italy has a very underrated railway in my view. The Köln-Frankfurt high-speed line is brilliant too - it follows a motorway through hilly terrain, and as you coast along at 300km/h (186mph), across viaducts and through tunnels, you leave the cars looking almost motionless on the road beside you.

Finally, it makes me laugh when Germans lay into Deutsche Bahn. It's a national pastime to bash the railway. Yet it seems much better than in many other European countries. Anyway – your hot take on DB, please!

DB does a lot with very little. Germany subsidizes its railway a lot less per head of population than neighbouring countries, but it still runs a lot of trains on this network that is by now, due to the lack of investment, literally falling apart in some places.

Germans tend to be highly critical of their railways, and of Deutsche Bahn as the main operator in particular, but I still maintain that DB does a better job for a lot more people of varying backgrounds and different financial means than lots of other railways do. I'm much more of a fan of what DB does than I am of SNCF or [Spain's] Renfe! Also, if you book ahead, you can still get crazy cheap deals on DB tickets - 25 euro for Berlin to Freiburg is a great deal. Sure, there are things Germany could do better - reliability has been poor in recent years, and is statistically worsening. But in the end you get what you pay for.

The nine-euro ticket in Germany in 2022. Good idea?

Those crazy three months where you could travel anywhere on regional trains for next to no money were a lot of fun. And simply making regional rail so cheap and simple to use was a radical change from the railway policy of the past. It also in particular benefitted low-income groups who previously could not afford public transport beyond the limits of their town or city.

But it's worth taking a step back and asking: what was the nine-euro ticket *for*? It was, after all, born of a political compromise – the liberals (FDP) in the government demanded a reduction of fuel tax, and the Greens (Die Grünen) said: 'Well, what about public transport users?' – but no one really stopped to ask what the precise purpose of the policy was. If it was to get people out of cars onto trains it did not work – but then who changes their behaviour based only on a three-month-long experiment?

Now there's a permanent 49-euro ticket instead – this one is designed to make permanent change, to get people to abandon their cars and use trains (and other public transport) for commuter trips instead. It is not as joyously cheap as the nine-euro ticket, but it might actually have a better chance of making some permanent change to behaviour than the nine-euro ticket did.

METRO

Bilbao, Spain

Looking like glass vials inserted into the earth, the entrances to Bilbao's Metro stations by Foster + Partners stand out in the otherwise brown and grey surrounds of Bilbao, the linear city in a valley dominated by industry which went on a mad 90s rebrand. The Guggenheim was part of this turnaround too, but the long red Metro line was also a clear attempt to use architecture to make people see the city differently. The industrial-inspired station mezzanines and unity of branding and design give it a crisp feel. Those escalator canopies and entrances are the real calling card though.

SKOPJE STATION

Skopje, North Macedonia

The clock on the old station lies forever stopped at 5.17, the time on 26 July 1963 when a massive earthquake destroyed almost the entire North Macedonian capital (then part of Yugoslavia, of course). The new city rose to a Kenzō Tange plan with the most extravagant and gallant metabolist intent and brutalist outcomes. Large parts of this golden age have now been turned into a weird theme park with the concrete covered over in Neo-classical façades, making it look like Vegas. The train station has so far survived this de-modernization. It is muscular with large expanses of concrete and space-age tubes and roofs hinting at what was planned by Tange to be an even more futuristic city.

WARSAW MODERNIST STATIONS

Warsaw, Poland

The war-ravaged streets of Warsaw were ripe for rebuilding and the post-war PKP stations sing about a very particular era in Polish history – that communist era is one that many in Poland wish to forget and it's probably a miracle these stations survive. The almost-parabolic roof of Ochota Station looks like a bird in flight and reminds you of the famous Little Chef at Markham Moor with a similar swooping roof in the East Midlands countryside of England. Powiśle's beautiful former ticket booth, built between 1954 and 1963 by architects Arseniusz Romanowicz and Piotr Szymaniak, has been reborn as a bar. Centralna's roof also recalls birds' wings. A 2010s rejig here at the city's largest terminal has added more light, space and retail into the mix.

HELSINKI CENTRAL STATION

Helsinki, Finland

Helsinki Central Station is one of the oldest we cast our eyes over in this book, built in 1919. But it sneaks in because its form is future-facing. The wild detailing – statues by Emil Wikström on the front, and the architecture by Eliel Saarinen (father of Eero – who designed such transport marvels as the TWA Flight Center in New York and Dulles Airport, Washington, DC) combine to make something very special – one of Europe's greatest 20th-century stations. It has a style which sits between Art Nouveau and Deco, and yet is fresh and daring. The use of green copper to top off the sandy stone is lively and it's the perfect entrance to the Finnish capital if you've come from Tampere and the north.

HAUPT-BAHNHOF

Vienna, Austria

Vienna's South Station was for many years the main station of the city, but Westbahnhof also hosted main-line and long-distance trains. The HBF project creates a new main station that takes on the roles of the Westbahnhof and the Südbahnhof, which has now been merged into the HBF and exists just as a memory. The white roof creates a large, airy space and the finishes are typically well done and with Austrian efficiency in the signage, circulation, etc. There are plenty of places to pick up a wurst and it works well when you're waiting for your Railjet or Nightjet – ÖBB (Austrian Federal Railways) has made this station the hub of its new cross-Europe nocturnal services as night trains stage an unlikely comeback in this eco age. ÖBB also has one of the slickest of the state-run railways, rivalled of course by the Swiss.

KOHTA STATION

Kohta, Finland

If wood is the future of building then Aalto University's Wood Programme is the way the designers of the future will be learning their craft. Students on the programme came up with this radical-looking shelter for those waiting for their trains at the small stop of Kohta. It mixes modern with traditional and shows how a bit of imagination can liven up a drab station and how wood can be a useful architectural tool – it also brings the Finnish forest right down to the train tracks.

T-BANA
STATIONS

Stockholm, Sweden

Stockholm's T-Bana (Tunnelbana) stations
are a glorious riot of colours and motifs. Art
adorns each of them and they have a primal
feel, like they were hollowed out of the earth
by elves or something. Akalla, Stadion, Tensta
and Tekniska Högskolan all boast trippy,
easily enjoyed but not necessarily easily read
artworks all over their walls, and a sublime
subterranean setting. Handsome blue trains
and the simple blue 'T' logo at stations give
a visual integrity to the whole project, which
opened in 1950 but continues to expand.

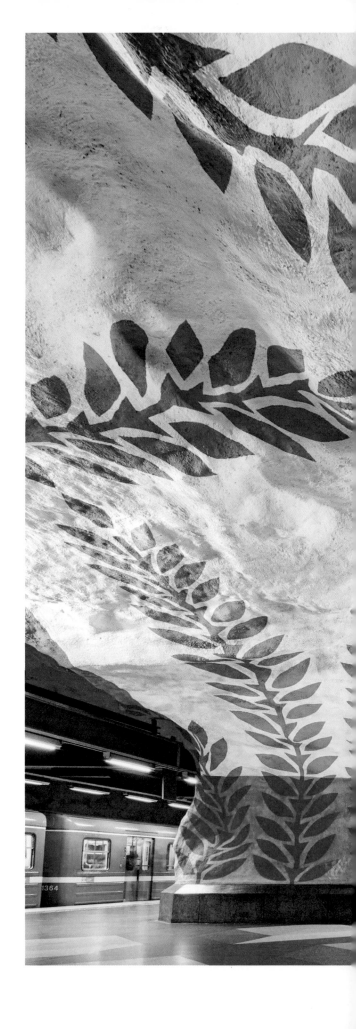

FROM
AEROTRAIN
TO TGV

France

France's dalliances with the sublime encompassed its out-of-the-box thinking on such things as Concorde and rubber-wheeled metro trains. The Aerotrain project of the 1960s essentially tried to put a hovercraft on a monorail track, with brilliant, Jetsons-esque vehicles going like the clappers. These didn't come to pass, sadly, but the country pioneered high-speed rail in Europe with the TGV, originally from Paris to Lyon, and with a killer colour scheme of orange, white and brown in its first incarnation (I had a toy version of this one). For the TGV schemes, station upgrades were completed across the SNCF network and new high-speed stations added like the Calatrava-designed one at Lyon Airport, which resembles a bird in flight. Now TGV lines have spread around France.

RER

Paris, France

The early 1970s attempt to take rail out to the suburbs in Paris was a reaction to the fact that the Metro really only served the (bourgeois) inner city while the new *banlieues* with their otherworldly modernist architecture were cropping up outside the Périphérique. The RER (Réseau Express Régional) provided quicker cross-city journeys and linked up to the new business district with its un-Parisian skyscrapers at La Défense. The stations are a product of their time – the arrival boards look classy with destinations flashing up, and the shop pods at Auber look like a Gauloises-chuffing and absinthe-smashing Pac-Man and his friends have run amok.

Jason Sayer

on the best modern station architecture

Jason Sayer is a critic, writer, and educator working in architecture. @jasonsayer

Tell us about the best modern architecture on the railways from the post-war era.

In the UK, the best stations that British Rail's regional architecture divisions gave us came in the form of Harlow Town, Coventry, Barking, Bedford Midland and, arguably the best, London Euston. These were (once) uncluttered, unfussy places that elegantly paired the graphical identity of BR with modernist architecture to create airy stations that instilled the sense that getting a train was, rightly, serious business. Sadly, many of these have been left unloved or have been picked at and prodded at almost beyond recognition, their original design intent a distant memory. Archive photos of Euston will paint a very different picture to what it is today.

In Italy, Rome's Stazione Termini embodied a similar approach to BR, as did the Santa Maria Novella in Florence, both with light-filled booking halls that boasted sumptuous clean lines to boot, the latter with a more Fascist inflection. Indeed, some of the best post-war station architecture can be found further abroad in Eastern Europe, and often at a smaller scale, as seen with the likes of Železnička Stanica Novi Sad in Serbia, Tulcea in Romania, the Warszawa Powiśle and Ochota in Warsaw, Poland, Zhytomyr in Ukraine, and Gyumri in Armenia.

Which stations and lines from the present day do you love and hate?

The High-Tech movement that emerged in the 1980s meant railway architecture could hark back to the stations of the Victorian era, rail's heyday, of which many were a tectonic tour de force, proudly expressing their structural skeletons. The new addition to Waterloo does this (I'll say more on that later), as does East Croydon. This ethos has been emulated elsewhere, at Lisbon's Oriente by Santiago Calatrava, who also was behind the glorious Liège-Guillemins in Belgium. Both are generously bathed in natural light and are structural spectacles. Honourable mentions also go to Rotterdam's Centraal Station, Berlin's Hauptbahnhof, Copenhagen's Nørreport Station, Napoli's Afragola Station and the 15-storey Kyoto Station.

Today, the worst stations encompass elements from the typology's arch-nemesis, the airport, being serene, soulless places of departure and arrival where the apparent main aim is to ensure you shop rather than catch your train, forcing you through a duty-free-style commercial onslaught instead of a platform. Birmingham New Street and Stratford (and Stratford International for that matter) are the worst offenders, in the UK at least.

The best line? The Pacific Surfliner service run by Amtrak traces the Californian coast, covering 565km (351 miles) between San Luis Obispo and San Diego. The West Coast weather seldom disappoints as well, so the view from the window will always be Hollywood-worthy.

Which architects did/do stations well?

Ray Moorcroft and Nick Derbyshire during their time at BR worked on some worthy projects, namely Euston and Waterloo in London, among many others. Although I've mentioned Calatrava already here, today perhaps the best in the business is Grimshaw Architects. Though I lament some of the changes being made to Euston Station (which the practice is modernizing), the studio's best work includes the likes of the former Eurostar terminus at Waterloo (on which Grimshaw worked with Derbyshire) – now used by suburban rail lines, which feels somewhat silly given how dowdy the trains are arriving amid the structural prowess on show painted in a brilliantly striking blue, which is a nice throwback to the great Victorian train sheds of more than a century ago. Grimshaw's Fulton Street Station in New York is often overlooked too – it has a brilliant oculus, and the modernization work at London Bridge also warrants note.

Why are trains so great – in your opinion?

Imagine finally getting the chance to travel to London and you land in Luton. With all due respect to the good folk of Luton, it's a horrific experience: you have to get a bus to an awfully dingy station which runs delayed services into actual London. Imagine, instead, you arrive at St Pancras Station. The glamour of travel (not just rail travel) abounds there – and in general, stations offer real architectural character as opposed to the sterile, hyper-secure airports of today, which don't even let you bring your own booze onboard.

Railway travel is inherently romantic, too. How can it not be when some services are named things like the Cornish Riviera Express (which will take you from Paddington to Penzance). Once you've escaped the city, hurtling along two lines of metal is both a thrilling and genuinely beautiful experience, particularly when you're cutting up the patchwork quilt that is the British countryside with the elegance and grace only locomotion can supply. Better still, when you look out of the window and find yourself storming past car after car.

OLYMPIA-ZENTRUM U-BAHNHOF

Munich, Germany

Opened for the 1972 summer Olympics in Munich, the station here on the U3 extension from the city centre was designed to bring fans to the Olympic Park. It echoes the brutalist athletes' village and Westin Hotel nearby and the tech-modernism of the BMW Tower and the stadium itself by Frei Otto. The wheels set in concrete on the station walls emphasize speed and movement. The orange signage and seating are set off by the grey raw concrete. Handsome blue Munich U-Bahn trains from a different era echo the whole picture. You can imagine a 100-metre runner puffing one last ciggie down here before heading up to compete.

U-Bahn Stations

in Berlin, Germany

The 1960s, 70s and 80s extensions of the U7, U8 and U9 in particular gifted West Berlin an array of pop/brutalist stations that each have a camp, space-station charm, and almost comprise a kind of Berlin transport 'style' that encompasses Tegel Airport, Berlin's International Congress Centre (ICC), various public offices and university campuses and the iconic Bierpinsel, which itself sits on top of Rathaus Steglitz Station – which is an explosion of colour and plastic that screams 1970s heroin heroism. Also by Rainer Rümmler, Fehrbelliner Platz has air vents and curves and decoration that seem postmodern. His vision for Konstanzer Strasse is like a 70s sleeveless V-neck pullover come to life and splattered on the station walls in orange, brown, yellow and beige.

Each station used different typefaces, tiles and colours of plastics. The only uniformity to it all was the guarantee you'd see someone smoking at whatever station you walked into. Schlossstrasse's pipes and ducts in primary colours by Ralf and Ursulina Schüler-Witte (also responsible for the ICC and Bierpinsel) makes you feel like you're under the bowels of a futurist space city where David Bowie would be playing a show.

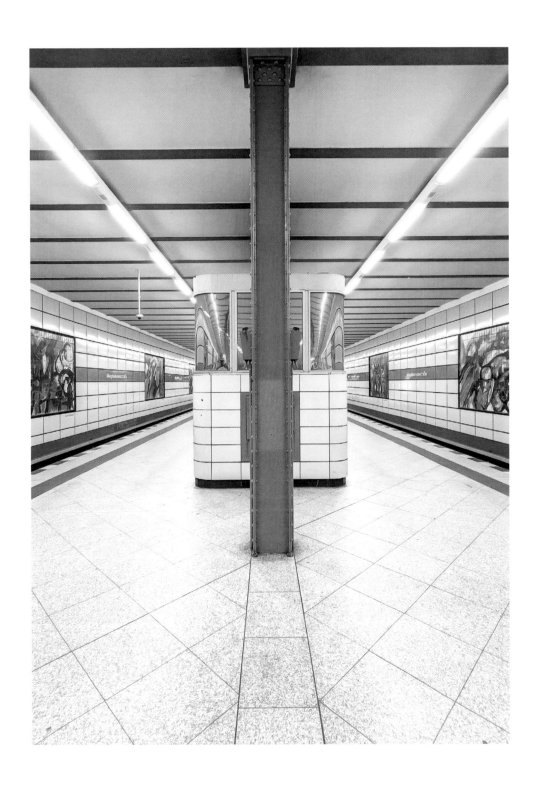

Magdalenenstrasse, Berlin U-Bahn.

Wittenau (Wilhelmsruher Damm), Berlin U-Bahn.

Berlin at the time of the U-Bahn extensions was of course divided, dilapidated and ready to party – it was also ready for these bonkers visions of the future, as outlined in Verena Pfeiffer-Kloss and Nigel Green's Blue Crow map of Berlin U-Bahn stations and a 2019 Berlinische Galerie exhibition on the 70 or so modern stations on the system, which was a neat follow-up to 2015's rabble-rousing Radikal Modern, which showed other progressive aspects of the city's rebellious post-war architectural legacy.

What's interesting about all this is that the new U-Bahn stations were almost entirely in the west of the city. The Communist East, whether by design or for a lack of funds (and the suspicion is probably the latter) never got around to building much beyond the U5 to Lichtenberg and Hönow. The East kept the trams and even today the U-Bahn map of Berlin somewhat mirrors the Underground map of London with almost no lines south of the Thames. In Berlin almost all the U-Bahn stations and lines were in the West as the trams here were torn up. But what replaced them was this plethora of different designs and intriguing architecture of the newer U-Bahn Stations.

The postscript to the saga is the most recent city addition – the U5 extension which finally links East and West down a new tunnel under Unter den Linden and connects the U-Bahn network to the Hauptbahnhof with some light and airy new stations.

BARNEVELD NOORD

Barneveld, Netherlands

Barneveld is the egg capital of the Netherlands and this is a cracking idea for a station. Cheap, new, boring stations often appear in Germany and the UK but here cheap is done with flair and sass. Old shipping containers have been flipped and used to create a simple modal solution at Barneveld Noord Nederlandse Spoorwegen Station - café, seats, ticket machine, toilet, clock. The model can be rolled out to any rural station, it looks great and has a little bit of a sense of humour about it too. Much better than most attempts to do this kind of thing on a budget.

IVANOVO STATION

Ivanovo, Russia

The first time I saw a picture of this station it leapt out at me and screamed. This is the one we all have to visit. I must confess, dear reader, that due to reasons you all know well enough this is not one I have been able to visit during 2022 or '23 – but I will. It looks absolutely remarkable; some say it's Russia's only remaining large constructivist station. The curves and streamed lines and glass look even more amazing because it was restored to its former 1930s glory during the Covid pandemic. It is the epitome of modern style, speed and pazazz. Inside, the wooden benches have been rehabilitated (they now come with plug sockets – in the 1930s you had to charge your iPhone at home). The hammer-and-sickle murals and mosaics and the blue-and-white painted waiting hall have all been brought back to life. It's a testament to the love of railways in Russia – the country depends on its trains. And in nearby Moscow, of course, there is one of the most fêted metro systems in the world – partly inspired by London's Underground.

AMERICAS

UNION STATION

Los Angeles, USA

It's Hollywood, baby – why wouldn't you get a glamorous station? Los Angeles's main rail terminal is a bubbly exercise in glitz. The unique orange arch you walk through on your way to the Amtrak trains makes it seem like you're walking onstage at the Oscars. The rows of leather seats are sumptuous. From outside, the Pueblo white façade with palm trees swaying in front is pure So-Cal cool. For so long forgotten, now LA's new rail renaissance has its heart here on the fringes of Downtown – reminding so many Americans that trains were such an unstoppable power before cars and planes stole their thunder. The idea of taking a train to New York now seems appealing again after years of decline, though that is easier said than done. But train trips around California are possible and LA's Metro line to Pasadena is not bad – it's just full of an array of quite colourful characters.

PEOPLE MOVER

Detroit, USA

What goes nowhere and has no riders? The Detroit People Mover's circular funfair tour of downtown Detroit's rooftops. Well, maybe there are more riders today as Detroit emerges from decades of malaise with a vigour and a population of can-do dreamers. And if they want to see the sights of the city centre, well, they can climb up to the stations like Huntington Place, pay their fare and wait for the one-way train to arrive. It'll take you to Greektown, where you can stuff your face with souvlaki in the places Jeffrey Eugenides used to hang out. And to the Renaissance Center, the huge John Portman towers headquartering General Motors. It's a neat joke that in the most car-centric city in the world, somehow this was built in the city centre. Let's celebrate that it's here – Sydney had a monorail loop too that was unceremoniously removed in 2002. We hope that doesn't happen. If people like Squarepusher, whose song and video 'Detroit People Mover' is a kind of homage, keep recognizing it, it should see at least a few more years of use.

METRO

Montreal, Canada

A series of brutalist bunkers lead down to the bowels of the city. If nothing else, use them when it's minus-20 degrees upstairs and you need to keep warm. The bolshy architecture is perfectly suited to its use and evokes a city that wanted to spread its wings in the 1960s with its Expo, the Habitat 67 housing complex, the huge Place Bonaventure (which also includes the city's main rail station) and the never-really-built Mirabel Airport complex. Distinctively shit but charming rubber-wheeled trains feel oh-so-Parisian and bizarre and make a weird noise when they approach. The system map looks *très* cool in black, like it was captured at night and inspired artwork for the band The Stills.

WASHINGTON DC METRO

Washington, DC, USA

Harry Weese's Metro architecture in
Washington, DC is almost perfect. It feels
dignified, civic, progressive and alluring. It's
dramatic and a bit weird and also very much
of its time, the first section opening in 1976.
The coffered ceilings and the lighting at
Metro Center make it feel like you've fallen
asleep after one too many chilli dogs from
Ben's Chili Bowl and woken up in a *Logan's
Run* sci-fi movie fever dream. The map, with its
thick coloured lines looks great, so does the
signage and logos. The brutalist aesthetics are
perfectly on point because – weirdly, perhaps
– although we think of the White House
and Congress and the 1800s architecture,
Washington is really a brutalist city, with
its government buildings, museums and art
galleries in unadorned raw concrete.

MOYNIHAN TRAIN HALL

New York, USA

Would Penn Station be torn down today? Of course not. We respect our heritage much more these days; we also value our railways. In the 1960s, though? Forget it. Robert Moses was in the ascendancy and it was all about bringing car parks and freeways into the centre of New York and every other American city. Trains were dying, the city was dying, a new arena was called for and Madison Square Garden was the plan. Penn Station was bulldozed so that Harry Styles could play 14 nights in a row 60 years later. The underground Penn Station was a disaster. To bring light, air and civilization into the station the Moynihan Train Hall finally offered redemption when it opened in 2019. It's a real pleasure to be here waiting for your new Acela train to the equally wonderfully Washington Union, enjoying the clock dangling down and the huge amounts of space. Food courts, shops, seats, wonderfully clean toilets – all the basics are done right. To create the new node the shell of the old US Mail Building across the road from the previous station was taken over – parasitically, perhaps – and the end result is as enjoyable as a pizza slice at midnight. The story continues, though, because the latest ruse is to take Madison Square Garden away and bring back a new version of the old Penn Station.

The Lowline
New York, USA

The silver doors slam shut and the M Train lurches off, piercing from underground darkness to twinkling autumnal sunlight, heading up and over the Williamsburg Bridge towards Marcy Avenue and Brooklyn's most hipster enclaves. The rest of the nonchalant travellers who have just detrained (as they say here) traipse towards the exit, leaving one very out-of-town-looking scribe on the platform at Essex Street.

The deserted, flaky paint scene reminds me of the movie *The Warriors*, where gangs chase round the Subway on one long, hot night. New York may have gentrified out of all recognition in the last 40 years, save for one creaking but essential part of the city: the subterranean world of the Subway, where the past has stood still. But change is coming below the Lower East Side's sidewalks. As the train slinks off, clattering and squeaking on the ageing tracks, a strange sight is revealed. A huge void sits alongside the station.

Depending on who you ask you could fit two swimming pools in here, or one football field, or I'd estimate around 500 very relaxed elephants. It looks like a warehouse – a massive space with pillars holding up the streets and clueless walkers above. This empty space will one day, in theory, become New York's newest attraction - the Lowline. The High Line is oversaturated with tourists, and its effect has also been to raise property prices - but then that happens whenever you do anything nice to an area.

So a new underground park, not affiliated with but certainly inspired by the creativity of the High Line, will be staking its claim for your time. This space is the former Williamsburg Bridge Trolley Terminal (trolley or streetcar is what Americans say; in British English it's a tram). The terminal lasted a paltry

40 years from 1908 to 1948 - streetcars from Brooklyn ran over the new Williamsburg Bridge and terminated on the underground platforms here before looping round for their return journey, while passengers could easily transfer onto the Subway. If the streetcars had remained, of course, the city would have had a golden nugget of public transport over the East River but, as happened in so many American and British cities, they were tossed in the trash, the victim of history's clearest conspiracy by the car industry to get rid of them.

The weird space remained empty and attracted dreamers and visionaries, like so many of these 'abandoned' underground stations. London's Down Street exerts a particular pull and Sydney's abandoned underground tunnels inspired a horror movie, *The Tunnel*. Now a motley crew of tech, culture and architecture geeks have had their interest piqued by the Williamsburg Bridge Trolley Terminal.

The finished park will cost $80m, feature a 10,000sq. ft (930sq. m) plaza and a 20,000sq. ft (1,860sq. m) garden. But how the hell will plants grow underground? Innovative solar panels, skylights and roof technology will make it feel less like a depot and more like a quiet oasis – and even perhaps a bit like

something you'd find on a space station. Just like with the High Line there'll be public art, seating and places to get coffee and snacks, as well as to wander. You might need to engage night mode on your iPhone to get the compulsory selfie though. There'll be toilets, shops and a lift from the surface down to the underground fun.

As the High Line popularized the use of old railway viaducts, maybe the Lowline could kick-start a trend for turning unused underground spaces into parks. Around the world there are hundreds of near-mythical spaces beloved of urban explorers that could work as parks. Paris's ghost stations like

Haxo, sealed-off underground car parks in London, Tirana's bomb-proof bunkers and Birmingham's many disused underpasses could all be candidates. Post-war Leeds had an eccentric network of underground passageways around the Merrion Centre and LA's many tunnels harboured speakeasies in the Prohibition era. Maybe parks are the future for these forgotten spaces.

Before that the Lowline needs to fill its space after first making safe the crumbling infrastructure. At the moment all you can see from the Essex Street platforms is a rather creepy, drippy tangle of metal supports, wires, puddles and bleakness. But, as they say on tiresome TV property shows, you really can see the potential for something eye-opening to bring light to the darkness down here, and to show the unconvinced that underground infrastructure can be as exciting to explore as that above our heads.

ORLANDO'S MONORAILS

Orlando, USA

Two visions captivated the chunkier, younger version of me on my first trip to the USA in 1990: the neon-clad stations of the people-movers that ferried passengers from the main terminal at Orlando Airport to the four satellite piers across watery flatlands and lakes; and, even more excitingly, the EPCOT Monorail's journey around the Walt Disney World Resort. The most satisfying station on this circuit is undoubtedly the one inside Disney's Contemporary Resort hotel – the whole building is by Welton Becket and Donald Wexler. The monorails sail into the 1971 lobby and stop to disgorge passengers as if it really were the future and *WALL-E* had come true. It's such a sight.

TORONTO
SUBWAY
EXTENSION
STATIONS

Toronto, Canada

The stations on the Spadina Subway Extension in Toronto have a jolly feel to them, characteristic of their fun-loving designer, the late great Will Alsop, who died after a life filled with fun and cigarettes, and a joyous, colour-filled attitude to architecture. Finch West and Pioneer Village display those sandbox-shaped tropes and the childlike and completely likeable attitude to colour that Alsop had. Bold, bright and enough to warm the cockles on a winter Ontario morning commute.

TREN MAYA

Mexico

One of Mexico's biggest ever infrastructure projects has been controversial from the start. A 1,000km (621 mile) railway carrying freight and passengers around the Yucatán Peninsula in a giant loop could eliminate flights and road journeys on one hand, but on the other increase tourism and threaten sensitive ecosystems and villagers, whose ancestors have lived and farmed in situ for hundreds of years. It's certainly a huge undertaking, with construction starting in 2020 and an anticipated opening date of December 2023. When this book is published in 2024 we will see whether that has come true! But judging by previous big rail projects, we might be left waiting. The station designs for stops like Tulum are infused with a little Latin flavour in the midst of the modernism and concrete.

MEXICO CITY METRO

Mexico

You might say this book is a compendium of some of the best stations and rail systems in the world. So why are we including a metro that might be considered the world's worst? The devastating crash of January 2023 and the bridge collapse of 2021 showed that Mexico City's Metro is extremely dangerous. The citizens of Ciudad de Mexico (CDMX as they call it) deserve better and the city needs to pull out its finger and repair the system rather than just deploying military and cops to the platforms and blaming the problems on saboteurs. While the fare varies from 6.50 to 15.50 pesos (much less than a pound or dollar) a go the coffers will be far from full, but then that cheapness means everyone can ride. I rode the rails here in 2023 and found a quirky and unique system. It's apt, as CDMX is a very likeable city filled with unbelievable architecture and design, though it, like its Metro, is creaking and faded. The 1970s stations with their marble and art displays were built as symbols of modernism. The astronomy display in the connecting tunnels at La Raza is a winner and the bespoke Metro DF font used for lettering is as bonkers as it is brilliant. The tangerine Paris Metro rubber-tyred trains clunked and grinded and their windows were covered in soot and grease, but I got back to the airport in one piece and for pennies, while getting to hang out with normal Mexicans on their way round town.

Mark Ovenden

on the beauty of subways, metros,
undergrounds and railway maps

Mark Ovenden is the author of Railway Maps of the World
and Metro Maps of the World.

**Tell us about your love of railway and
subway maps, Mark, and where that
came from.**

Some of my earliest memories involve maps.
Their magnetism offered clues to distant
unseen landscapes or, later, as flattened
reminders of poignant landmarks. There
were always maps in our west London home.
Outdated road maps cast down when Dad
acquired newer ones, Underground maps
thrust at us as toddlers by my mum in vain
hope we would fidget less en route to the
West End where Dad worked long shifts
as a chef, visiting relatives at Stanmore
on what was then the Bakerloo Line or to
Harrow-on-the-Hill via the Metropolitan.
Thousands of miles of railway branch lines –
resplendent on those older maps consulted
on car trips – had recently been brutalized
by the Beeching axe. As we clattered into

towns, villages and picturesque country
from South Wales valleys to New Forest
woodlands, the smooth Norfolk Broads
to the undulating Sussex Downs, gloomy
seaside resorts to optimistic new towns ... we
held in our hands a two-dimensional slice of
both past and present. Dad would drag us
along miles of windswept old rail trackbed.
Gradually I'd cherish seeking out the latest
Ordnance Survey 'dismntld rlwy' and could
trace the line of overgrowing embankments
and cuttings on the ground, even when the
written words had been dropped on later
editions of the maps as these lamented
losses became a distant memory. Why was
this street called 'Station Road' or that area
have a line of unwired telegraph poles?

Some forward-thinking art teachers allowed
me to write a project on the London

Underground, which helped me towards a sixth-form place with emphasis on art. As a result I doodled a topographical map; [a] geometrically accurate attempt at redesigning the sacred London Underground map. The messy spaghetti proved to me why those features had been removed by Harry Beck but got me a place at Southampton Art College for sheer nerve.

Although I then pursued a print, journalist and media career after this, I never lost my fascination for maps and continued collecting treasures from around the world until, after lending out my precious maps to mates (only to get many back with extra stains or creases on!), I decided to compile them into my first book: *Metro Maps of the World* (2003).

Which post-war maps are your favourite for railways and subways?

Depends on criteria, but favourite maps are Moscow (Central Circle captures the eye), London, Madrid, Barcelona (Beck-style). Most complex ones: Tokyo, Seoul, New York. Worst design: Mexico City (official map). Funniest: Sendai, Kobe.

Why is good design important with trains and railways and stations?

If an organization is going to the vast expense of building and operating a public transit system surely they want people to use it and like it. Design is core to functionality – I think it was Hans Hofmann who said, 'Design is the intermediary between information and understanding.' Massimo Vignelli, who conceived of the brilliant, classic 1970s

NYC Subway map, said: 'Good design is a language, not a style.' It's impossible to divorce the understanding of complex systems without good design: in a labyrinth maze of tunnels you'd quite simply be lost without good design. It must infuse the passengers' journey from maps to way-finding. Make it simple and they will come!

Favourite subway and railway stations around the world? Any brand-new ones you like and any from the late 20th century?

Washington Metro stations, London's Elizabeth Line, the stunning palaces of the Moscow Metro ... all shrines to urban rail transit architecture, but they do not have to be underground cathedrals to be well made and effective at moving masses of people in pleasant surroundings. Just make the spaces bright, easy to navigate and fit for purpose and that will make a good subway or railway station.

Favourite subway system and why?

Ha ha, well, there are so many wonderful – and also so many not so good – aspects it's quite hard to narrow it down. Also, sadly, I've probably been lucky enough to visit less than 10 per cent of the ones we now have on this planet – and absolutely none in the massively expanding area of Asia, so, my current faves are: Paris Metro (simply because there are so many stations so close together), London Underground (design heritage), Madrid Metro (much expanded and well designed), Washington, DC Metro (spacious stations), Barcelona Metro (more great design/maps).

MINIRAIL

Montreal, Canada

The most popular thing at Expo 67 wasn't any of the incredible pavilions – it was the infamous Minirail that trundled around the site, gave visitors panoramic views of the crazy architectural oddities and later featured in the video to Alvvays' dream pop single 'Dreams Tonite'. It was a long, snaking, fun train perched on a monorail, with overhead stops at the main sights. For no good reason the tracks and stations were lifted in 2022, but the whole piece was pure 60s silliness. It showed that trains and stations could and should be fun – and was the missing link between grown-up railways and their many theme park cousins.

MASSIMO VIGNELLI NYC SUBWAY SIGNAGE AND MAP

New York, USA

The signage on the New York Subway system has become iconic – emblazoned on clothing and posters and starring in photos. The station name signs, entrance signs and, more crucially, direction signs within stations look slick in white on black Helvetica, the arrows point the right way and the coloured line bullets do their best to help tourists understand this most complex of systems, which was a total mess before the new signage came in. Massimo Vignelli and Bob Noorda (and Massimo's wife Lella) also came up with a London Underground-esque simplified diagram in 1972, but this map only lasted a decade before a more retrograde one came in. The whole programme revolutionized the Subway and started it on a long, slow road to recovery – today it is widely used and if not exactly loved then certainly essential, well maintained and there for you whenever you need it.

ANAHEIM TRANSIT CENTRE

LA, USA

Finally, a grown-up station to encourage public transit use in one of the most car-loving and consumerist cities on Earth, a place where – unlike in other major cities – public transit still has a huge image problem and the car is king. LA had dozens of streetcar lines until the Great Streetcar Conspiracy ended that. But rail is staging a comeback and the pillowy-roofed station here in the suburb of Anaheim (famous of course for its Mighty Ducks) is a symbol of that growth, with its airy and simple design by HOK. It also connects to buses and the city's Metro rail as well as Amtrak mainlines.

SÃO PAULO METRO

São Paulo, Brazil

Boasting one of the coolest logos of any metro system, the up-and-down arrows of the São Paulo Metro look as swish and 70s as a pair of bell bottoms. The original trains looked like they had graduated from the University of Cool with their sloping fronts, off-centre window and logo emblazoned. The 70s brutalist stations of the original incarnation went in tandem with the likes of Lina Bo Bardi's buildings in the metropolis and no one could argue that sprawling São Paulo did not need this system to help weary citizens get around town. Further expansions have produced more interesting modern stations and graphic design across Brazil's biggest city, and lots of art in stations too.

The Calatrava Effect

The dinner-party discussion topic for architecture/train geeks: do we love a Santiago Calatrava train station or has he lost the plot? His City of Arts And Sciences in Valencia is not a train station but is one of the most complained-about buildings in modern memory, where locals gather to shout about how awful they think it is. The arrivals area at Bilbao Airport is a bad joke: you're spat out on the street, thinking, 'Is someone taking the piss?'

The stations? Well, waiting at Liège-Guillemins in the winter is not for the faint of heart – as with Bilbao, you wish the outside was, if not inside, then with a few old-fashioned things like, ooh, walls, to protect you from a biting breeze.

This station on the Brussels to Cologne high speed line is a sight that instantly grabs your attention when you make a stop on an international ICE train. We wonder what regular travellers make of its 'look at me' drama, like an Instagram influencer out for likes at any cost.

Lisbon Oriente needs some TLC. Built for the 2006 Expo, it is looking a little grotty. But as with all architecture – it's all about the caretaking. Those white surfaces need a lot of upkeep – this is another reason why the idiotic painting of brutalist concrete is stupid too. Oriente was the hub for the Expo site and remains a big part of Portugal's train system, a system which is not

The Oculus, World Trade Center Transportation Hub, New York, USA.

Reggio Emilia AV Mediopadana, Italy.

quite as bold as that of other European countries. But it's getting there and Lisbon is also gradually extending its little Metro, which is costing a fortune but will make this cool city even easier to get around.

Lyon Saint-Exupéry TGV brings the airport to the railway line with some panache. The station thinks it's a bird or something and looks stunning in the morning sunshine; the links between train and plane are subtly played with. It's an impressive feat, perhaps Calatrava's best station design.

The biggest and newest folly is the Oculus in New York, which has a kind of use as a Subway and PATH station – though try finding the trains. It presents itself more as a kind of neutral space, with shops surrounding a cathedral-like interior, where people often practise yoga outside CVS, and the spindly top looks like it took its cues from Lyon (and Valencia) and of course archaeology, as with the other buildings Calatrava does. As they say: if it ain't broke, don't fix it ...

Functional? Pah. Fun? Go on then, why not. At least it's all distinctive.

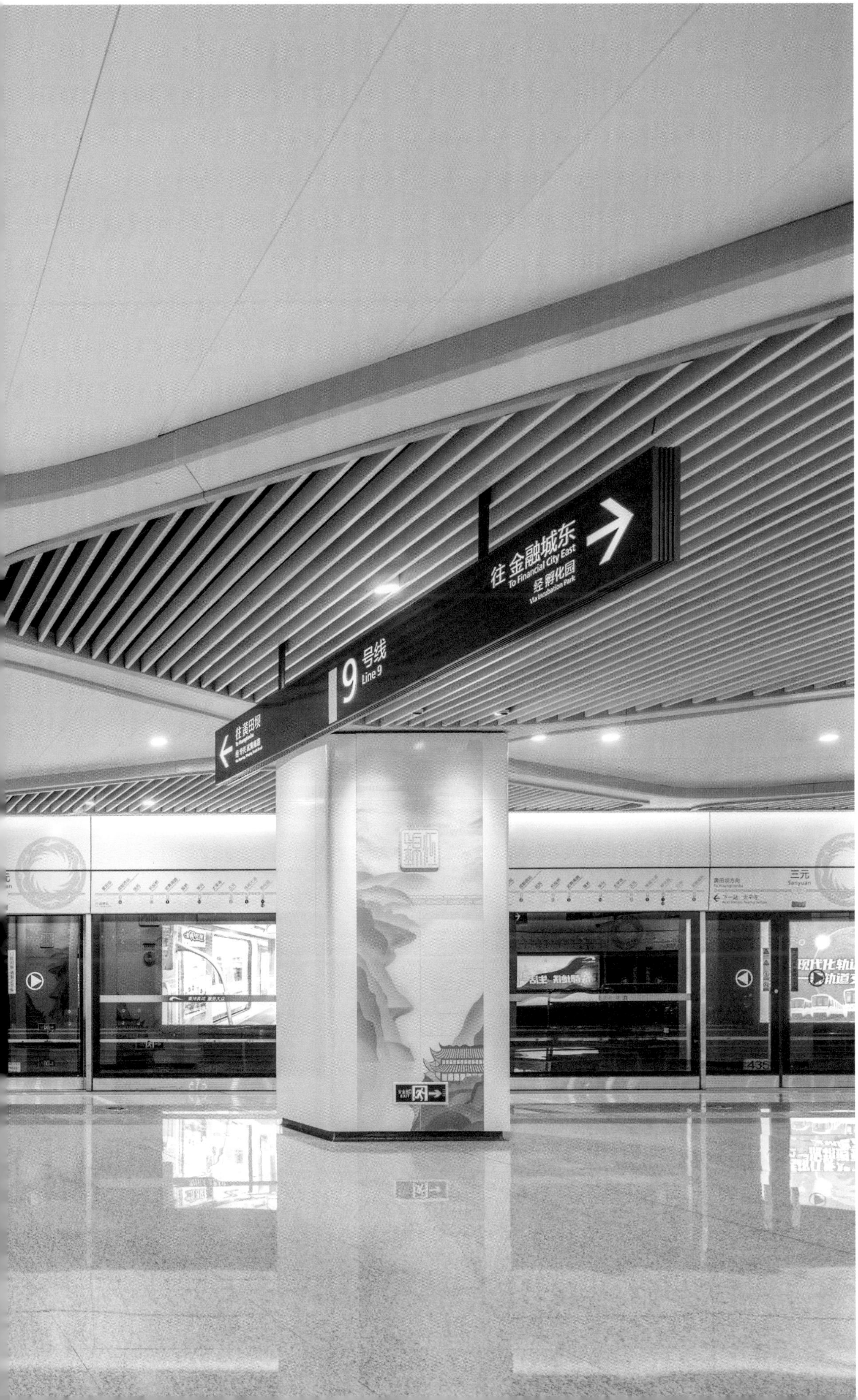

REST OF THE WORLD

MAIN STATION

Taipei, Taiwan

Constructed for the opening of the high-speed line which runs down the western spine of this remarkable and beautiful island that few really understand, Taipei's central station is a solid edifice that does its job in an un-shouty way. The station box has a high roof letting light in, plenty of retailers purveying bubble tea and bento-esque boxes for hungry travellers about to head down to Taichung, Tainan and beyond on the country's own bullet train, and despite being busy it's never too stressful. Metro lines and local trains converge here too but it's never too much.

EASTERN SUBURBS LINE

Sydney, Australia

Budgie smugglers? Check. Slab of coldies? Check. Surfboard? Check. You'll need to get yourself out to the beach now. The best way to avoid Sydney's traffic? On the Eastern Suburbs Line. This one should not even be up for our consideration as a 'modern' addition to the railway – it should have always been a central part of the Sydney railway network whose 1950s city-centre loop line was inspired by the New York Subway and features a ton of secret tunnels and pleasingly retro stations underneath Hyde Park. However, as with the Opera House, this one took an eternity to complete after years of delays in the planning and construction. Finally, in 1979, the whole thing opened. Well, we say the 'whole' thing – you'll immediately wonder why you're still miles from the beach when you're belched up to the surface at Bondi Junction with a Westfield shopping mall looming over you. What do we like on this line? The graphics are cool – the big wide words of each station sign on the platform, the architectural legacies of the time like the curves in the windows you can see at Martin Place and, most intriguing, the ghost-station platforms at Woollahra between Bondi Junction and Edgecliff, where the station construction was stopped due to budgets running out and local opposition to the stop. Today in Sydney the biggest new railway is the cross-city Metro which opens, in theory, in 2024.

Mark Smith

on the joys of long-distance
train travel around the world

*Mark Smith is The Man In Seat 61 (seat61.com)
– his chosen seat on the Eurostar.*

Tell us briefly why you like train travel.
I love seeing what's over the next hill, different
cultures, cuisines, places, history. And when
you travel, it's not just a destination, it's also
about the journey. And if you want a journey
where you're treated like a human being, can
see where you're going, can sleep in a bed,
can eat in a restaurant, can stand up and
move around – that means train or ship. I also
feel a connection with history when I travel by
train or ship, not so by air.

**We're looking at newer rather than
older stations in this book. Any from
after 1945 to the present you've liked
on your travels around the world?**
Berlin HBF and Vienna HBF stand out as
modern terminals for capital cities, both
replacing multiple termini with a single,
central through station, and both are nice

places to be. While I admire Santiago
Calatrava's beautiful architecture at Liège-
Guillemins and Lisbon Oriente, they are
draughty stations from a passenger's point
of view and not such nice places to wait for
a train! That said, Lyon Saint-Exupéry is also
spectacular, without the draughts.

**Which modern stations in the
UK do you love and loathe?**
The station everyone loves to hate is
Birmingham New Street – not without
reason. But after its recent facelift it's much
improved, at least before you descend to the
platforms. The rebuilt station at Blackfriars
deserves a mention, with platforms spanning
the Thames with glass walls giving superb
views as you wait for your train. And the
newly facelifted Glasgow Queen Street also
deserves a pat on the back.

Any cool railway design you've stumbled on around the world?

In Indonesia, the best day and night trains between Jakarta and Surabaya feature airline-style business-class flatbeds with flat-screen TVs. Meanwhile, new sleeper trains being built for Europe's Nightjet sleeper network will feature private 'mini-suites' modelled on Japanese capsule hotels, offering a bed in a private space for an economy fare. The ability to put vinyls on train exteriors has led to many special liveries, including the Pride trains here in the UK, and advertising liveries for this or that. But please, operators, not over the windows!

How can we make cross-border journeys more seamless and attractive?

We need sensible track access charges, recognizing (for example) that sleeper trains have more difficult economics than other trains, and that the marginal cost of an extra train on an existing line is close to zero. We also need better passenger rights – to guarantee onward travel even if a delay means a missed connection, even where the journey is being made on separate tickets with different operators. Unlike air, rail is a network, and must be seen as such. And we need better booking systems that can book multiple trains and operators in one place. At present every operator has its own system and booking systems are fragmented.

METRO
STATIONS

Doha, Qatar

Gleaming and encompassing Arabic touches and clean, white modernism, Doha's new Metro stations epitomize this confusing city set between the past and the future. Doha has spent big on 'starchitecture' – I. M. Pei's Art Gallery and Jean Nouvel's flying saucer Museum of Qatar. The stations of the new Metro were built for the most controversial football World Cup ever, staged in the winter of 2022 and dogged by lack of LGBTQ+ rights and the sacrifices of the workers who built the stadia – and the Metro stations. They at least try to get the car-addicted country on the rails and heading for a better future of rail journeys.

TOKYO SHIBUYA STATION AND MŌKA STATION

Honshu Island, Japan

A tale of two stations, big and small. Shibuya is not the prettiest but certainly a key experience in understanding modern Tokyo and how it came to be so reliant on the rails. Shibuya Station is that chaotic first crush: you don't know why you like them and you can't understand them, but you always end up going back. The nature of the levels of the city made me think a lot the first time I was here – I puzzled at how the motorway, the pedestrian layers, the tracks, the platforms, the bridges, the concourses, all seemed to fit among each other like a puzzle. The statue of the famous dog Hachikō who kept waiting here for nine years after his owner's death is a tourist attraction, as is the head-spinning Shibuya Crossing outside the station. Recent renovations have brought more space to the station complex. At the other end of the spectrum, behold the gloriously bonkers Mōka Station in the countryside north of Tokyo. Shaped exactly like a steam train and dating from the 1990s, it is a postmodern fever dream. It is certainly nothing unusual in a country that has trains filled with bonsai gardens and elsewhere paints its trains like cats – and employs felines as stationmasters.

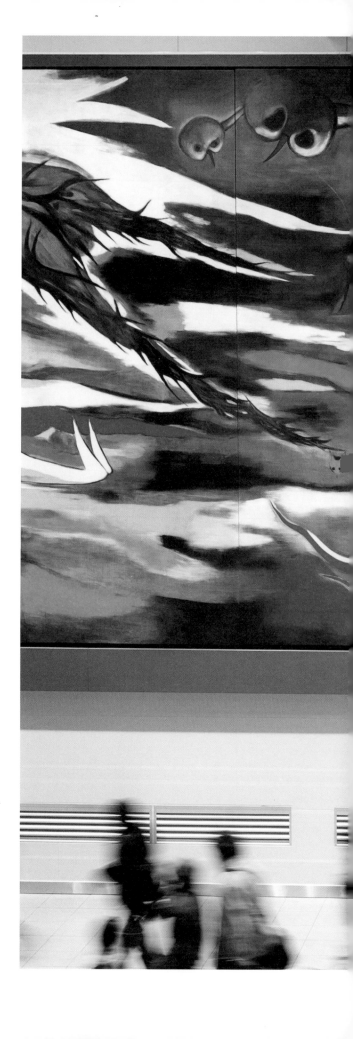

SOUTHERN CROSS AND FLINDERS STREET STATIONS

Melbourne, Australia

It looks more like a market hall or Polish airport terminal from the outside, but once you realize it's one of Melbourne's primary transport nodes, you're on your way to understanding Southern Cross and its hold on the city. The 2000s rejig was an attempt to refine the 1960s redevelopment of a Victorian steam palace - it's almost out of the same handbook as Birmingham New Street in the UK. The connection bridges over to Docklands are handy and switching between the city's great trams and trains is easier. And in a country where the car is king, anything to get people on the rails has to be welcomed. Maybe Aussies are loving stations again - a 2023 installation inside nearby Flinders Street's upper levels and ballroom that had been hidden for decades by artist RONE was a hit in the city and emphasized the romantic history of these buildings.

GUANGZHOU SOUTH STATION

Guangzhou, China

With a huge footprint and massive amounts of space, Guangzhou South is one of China's primary train stations and one of Asia's largest railway hubs. The 2010 station by Farrells (who have basically rebuilt China) has that characteristic modern and light vibe at odds with the heaviness of the materials and the trains that use it. You can travel all over the country on China's many high-speed lines – lines, trains and stations that put the West to shame in how fast and with how much ambition they were all slotted together. Across China there are many more of these new stations, especially on the new high-speed network.

HARAMAIN LINE

Saudi Arabia

Saudi Arabia's high-speed Haramain Line, travelling down the west coast of the country from Medina to Mecca via Jeddah, is another example of big railway projects in the Gulf, along with Dubai and Doha's Metro systems. Here four new super-stations with Arabian design twists serve as stops on the partly Spanish-engineered line, with architecture designed to withstand the desert heat from Foster + Partners. Each station is built on a grand scale – this country is into supersized projects, from huge aerotropolis airports to the questionable Neom/The Line – a new linear city. Whether these projects should really be built is a moot point – certainly more care and attention need to be given to both environmental concerns and local populations in the midst of these builds, but that is a global problem, not just a local one.

VIENTIANE STATION

Vientiane, Laos

The biggest and most important station on the Laos–China high-speed line, which opened in late 2021, Vientiane is a shiny addition to the city and a marker of how far previously struggling and landlocked Laos has come. The line is, of course, part of a Chinese soft-power offensive, with funding and engineering know-how coming over the border from Beijing, and a direct connection to China's railways that makes trade between the countries more seamless as part of the 'belt and road' initiative. The station's brown roof nods to the local vernacular, and to the 'city of sandalwood' as Vientiane is known, while its glassy walls are standard station modern.

Hanging Railways
Germany, USA, Japan

Some of the weirdest and most wonderful of the railway variations we see around the world are the hanging railways. These were like something concocted by H. G. Wells. Here the train was suspended below the tracks, which themselves were elevated up in the sky. One was trialled in Glasgow during the Victorian era. Others popped up around the world in theory and even sometimes in practice.

The most famous is at Wuppertal, Germany where the Schwebebahn (or hanging railway) tracks run above the city's river and the stations are up on high platforms (with barriers to stop riders plunging into the icy waters or streets below). This line has become the de facto symbol of the city. It swings and swoops along the river valley, its engaging mixture of vintage and modern looking backwards and yet forwards at the same time. The cars dangling below the tracks seem like everything is the wrong way round, upside-down like in *The Twits*. You can't fail to find it all exhilarating. The elaborate iron structures could have gone the same way as New York's extensive 'L' elevated Subway lines, which were torn down across

The Wuppertal Schwebebahn (Wuppertal Suspension Railway), Germany.

The Shonan Monorail, Enoshima, Japan.

Manhattan in the 20th century, but the Germans persisted with this oddity in the Ruhr and the result is well worth a ride.

Manchester wanted to build one to its airport in the 1960s and Düsseldorf actually did this, linking its Deutsche Bahn airport train station and airport terminal and airport car parks. It's an exciting way to transfer from train to plane and makes for a trio of fun transport experiences in a single day. The French suspended SAFEGE test track features in Truffaut's film of *Fahrenheit 451*.

The swing of the cars is a fun added touch, plus the sensation of 'flying' you get when riding on one of these. Japan embraced the technology with the Shonan Monorail and one at Ueno Zoo.

Chiba also boasts a long version of this idea.

There was one at the 1964 World's Fair in New York. Dallas Love Field Airport in the USA operated one in the early 1970s and in the 1980s Memphis built a system to link to the Mud Island Park in the Mississippi where, in a meta twist, there is a scale model of the river next to the real river. This cherry-red one lies forlorn and ready for a restoration. A version was briefly trialled in Margao, India, in the 2010s too.

In 2022 a new hanging monorail line opened in Wuhan, China – hoping to make that particular city known for something other than you know what. And in Ganzhou they've gone one better – a brand-new suspended maglev line.

TAKANAWA GATEWAY

Tokyo, Japan

The roof of the new Takanawa Gateway Station was inspired by Japanese origami papercraft and the whole building is flooded with light from the exuberant use of glass in the roof and walls. The finishes are crisp and expensive like a corporate office block. It's no wonder it looks so good – maestro Kengo Kuma was behind the design and so it really does appear as a cut above the quotidian. The new station opened in 2020 and serves the Yamanote Line in Tokyo. Tokyo's many stations are always clean but usually rather cramped, and this one points the way towards a slightly less congested vision of the future. Situated south of Tokyo's core and near the water of Tokyo Bay, the station was needed (so it was thought) for the Tokyo Olympics of 2020 – the Games no one showed up for. But a nearby urban regeneration project will assure its future as a useful node.

Laura Millar

on Ninja and Harlequin
trains in Japan and Italy

Laura Millar is travel editor of Metro UK.

Tell us briefly why you like train travel.
I didn't set foot on a plane till I was 18, so my formative travel years took place in cars and on trains. I love the relaxed feeling of just sitting back, letting the scenery unfold, and getting stuck into a book (or, more likely these days, some work, annoyingly). It feels very peaceful, calming and unfrenetic.

Any modern stations you've liked on your travels around the world?
I have been by train from Tokyo to Kyoto, and Kyoto Station is relatively new (or has been rebuilt, at least). It's all glass and steel and quite futuristic; a suitable and striking contrast to the city and all its ancient temples.

Which modern stations in the UK do you love and loathe?
The only one I can think of is Stansted, which is post-1945; and I only 'love' it because it grants access to the airport!

Do you think high-speed rail is a good idea – HS2, etc.?
In theory, yes; Japan's bullet trains are incredible, for example. But then they built their train system after the UK's creaky old one so it's no real surprise it's efficient and fast. Let's see if HS2 actually works (or even gets completed!).

Any cool graphics/logos, cool or weird trains you've stumbled on abroad?

I went on a 'Ninja' train in Japan, which goes to the forests of the Iga Province where ninja used to train. It's covered in cute cartoon pics of ninjas. And there's a train in Italy called the Arlecchino ('Harlequin'), dating from the 1960s, which has just been restored and looks incredibly cool – hoping to get on that at some point.

Are travellers going to give up flying for trains in the future?

I'd like to think they'll use trains more and planes less, particularly for journeys between the UK and Europe – the new sleeper route from Brussels to Berlin, for example, is encouraging. But it will take more time. Hopefully now that working is a bit more flexible, people could use the journey to work rather than have to take too much time off.

CANBERRA STATION

Singapore

This 2019 addition to Singapore's sleek MRT (Mass Rapid Transit) subway system is named after Australia's capital city. Its theme is maritime, with the nearby docks once hosting British naval vessels. The ship-shaped station building with a proud prow roofline looks ready to sail off into the sunset. The architects have won plaudits for their use of natural materials and plants in an attempt to make the building eco-friendly. This use of green stuff is a big thing in Singaporean transport design – just look at Changi Airport, which is also rich in plant life and water features.

LINE 9

Chengdu, China

Silkworm cocoons and lotus flowers are some of the inspirations for the flashy designs of the new Line 9 stations on the Chengdu Metro. A bright white palette is accentuated by colour coding of individual stations – yellow, green, etc. – in this design by China's J&A and the UK's Sepanta. The 22km (13 ¾ mile) Metro line stretches through the city of Chengdu and the stations echo the kind of Chinese style of white modernism you can see at Shenzhen Airport and the natural-world-influenced wavy lines epitomized by MAD's Harbin Opera House.

INDIA'S EVOLVING RAILWAY STATIONS

India

The Indian rail network is famed as one of the world's densest and most heavily used. The country takes trains very seriously and its railway company is one of the world's biggest entities. In 2022 the government announced a huge plan to revamp 200 stations. New buildings will be popping up all over India as the creaking system drags itself into the 21st century. Byappanahalli in Bengaluru (Bangalore) is an air-conditioned, spacious station that opened in 2022 and looks like an airport terminal. The plans for the hub station at the capital, New Delhi, are even more out there: domes and towers and acres of space a world away from the chaos of the current Indian railway station – a chaos that is nevertheless oddly satisfying in a way, with street vendors flogging samosas and memories of Wes Anderson's *The Darjeeling Limited* hanging in the air. But the future looks bright for India's stations.

ABOUT THE AUTHOR

Christopher Beanland writes comedy, novels (*The Wall in the Head* and *Spinning out of Control*) and non-fiction books (*Lido, Unbuilt, Concrete Concept, City Parks*). He also presents the podcast Park Date.

Follow Christopher and get in touch:

Instagram: Christopherbeanland

Twitter: Chrisbeanland

christopherbeanland.com

Park Date podcast is available on

Spotify, Audible, Apple Podcasts and all podcast providers

Instagram, Twitter, TikTok: Parkdatepodcast

parkdate.co.uk

THANK YOU

Helen Coffey, David Lawrence, David Ellis, Christian Wolmar, Nigel Green, Jason Sayer, Dan Elkan, Simon Calder, Tim Dunn, all at Brown Bob, Laura Millar, Mark Smith, all at *The Independent*, Frida Green, Nicola Newman, Lilly Phelan and all at Batsford.

FURTHER READING

The Modern Station: New Approaches to Railway Architecture
Brian Edwards
(Routledge, 2016)

Stations
Chris van Uffelen
(Braun Publishing, 2010)

The Railroad Station: An Architectural History
Carroll L. V. Meeks
(Dover Publications, 2012)

Design: Vignelli: Graphics, Packaging, Architecture, Interiors, Furniture, Products
Beatriz Cifuentes-Caballero
(Rizzoli, 2018)

Railway Maps of the World
Mark Ovenden
(Penguin Books, 2012)

Geoff Marshall
(YouTube)

The Architecture the Railways Built
(UKTV Play)

CAPTIONS FOR CHAPTER OPENERS

Pages 18–19: Docklands Light Railway (DLR) train, Canary Wharf, London
Pages 58–59: Munich Marienplatz, Munich, Germany
Pages 116–117: Metro Center Station, Washington, DC, United States
Pages 160–161: Line 9, Chengdu, China

PICTURE CREDITS

INDEX